MANAGEMENT'S GUIDE TO SARBANES-OXLEY SECTION 404

MAXIMIZE VALUE WITHIN YOUR ORGANIZATION

Norman Marks, CPA, CRMA

Published by The Institute of Internal Auditors Research Foundation

247 Maitland Avenue

Altamonte Springs, Florida 32701-4201

The Institute of Internal Auditors' (IIA's) International Professional Practices Framework (IPPF) comprises the full range of existing and developing practice guidance for the profession. The IPPF provides guidance to internal auditors globally and paves the way to world-class internal auditing.

The IIA and The IIARF work in partnership with researchers from around the globe who conduct valuable studies on critical issues affecting today's business world. Much of the content presented in their final reports is a result of IIARF-funded research and prepared as a service to The IIARF and the internal audit profession. Expressed opinions, interpretations, or points of view represent a consensus of the researchers and do not necessarily reflect or represent the official position or policies of The IIA or The IIARF.

ISBN-13: 978-0-89413-810-2

18 17 16 15 14   2 3 4 5 6 7 8 9

CONTENTS

About the Third Edition and the 2013 Update

THIS IS AN updated, significantly expanded version of The Institute of Internal Auditor's (IIA's) *Sarbanes-Oxley Section 404: A Guide for Management by Internal Controls Practitioners.* Changes include:

- Updates to reflect the 2013 version of the Committee of Sponsoring Organizations of the Treadway Commission's (COSO's) *Internal Control – Integrated Framework.*

- Updated references to the U.S. Public Company Accounting Oversight Board's (PCAOB's) Auditing Standard No. 5, *An Audit of Internal Control Over Financial Reporting That Is Integrated With an Audit of Financial Statements* (AS 5), the newer Auditing Standard No. 11, *Consideration of Materiality in Planning and Performing an Audit,* and the U.S. Securities and Exchange Commission's (SEC's) *Guidance Regarding Management's Report on Internal Control Over Financial Reporting Under Section 13(a) or 15(d) of the Securities Exchange Act of 1934.* The first edition was based on the top-down, risk-based approach adopted in these documents, and the second edition updated the discussion and extended the guidance provided by the regulators.

- An expanded discussion of IT general controls scoping based on The IIA's Guide to the Assessment of IT Risk (GAIT) series.

- An extended discussion of the role of entity-level controls.

- New content related to the:

  - International versions of the U.S. Sarbanes-Oxley Act of 2002.

  - Use of technology in the Sarbanes-Oxley program.

- Relationship between Sarbanes-Oxley; governance, risk management, and compliance (GRC); and enterprise risk management (ERM).

- Improving the efficiency of the system of internal control over financial reporting (ICFR).

- Working with the external auditor.

- The role of the internal auditor.

- The benefit of additional years of experience with management's assessment of ICFR.

The approach discussed in this guide has proven successful over the last few years—streamlining management's process and effecting major reductions in total assessment cost.

WHAT PEOPLE SAY ABOUT THE THIRD EDITION:

"Norman Marks continues his contribution to the profession with his dogged focus on risk assessment as the linchpin for scoping governance processes and control reviews. His pragmatic approach can assure corporate leaders that Sarbanes-Oxley frameworks can be efficient, effective, and value added as opposed to simply regulatory overhead, driving more inspection and documentation just because more is better. Assurance practitioners themselves can use Marks' approach to ensure their audit efforts focus on the critical needs of internal and external stakeholders and thus free up scare resources to tackle other critical enterprise risks."

— James Rose, Vice President, Internal Audit

"This book will help many future public company professionals in the important aspect of Sarbanes-Oxley—understanding the requirements, nuances, and approach before you have to do it. It will also help veterans to challenge and validate their existing approach to ensure it is tightly and correctly constructed and considers many helpful suggestions."

— Robert Hirth, Executive Vice President, Protiviti

"Sarbanes-Oxley has become a routine process at many companies. Leading edge companies are using this new guide to lean out the Sarbanes-Oxley process; reducing the cost of compliance while improving the overall quality of the program. This updated guide is a great tool for those employees who are new to Sarbanes-Oxley, its history, and its requirements. The guide gets them totally up to speed while giving them leading edge thoughts about how they can lean out the process and improve the quality of the program at the same time."

— Larry Harrington, Vice President, Internal Audit,
Raytheon Company

"Overall, I found this to be a very useful, well-organized and well-written guide. I particularly like the focus on management's responsibility and the imperative to drive overall efficiency, along with concrete guidance on how to do so. Too much Sarbanes-Oxley guidance is directed toward the external auditor, leaving management to either extrapolate from, or worse, take direction from the external auditors on program design and operation. So, a great perspective and very useful to management if IIA can publicize more broadly than just to internal auditors. The real-world examples really enhanced the readability/understanding."

— Rod Winters, General Manager,
Finance Operations, Microsoft Corporation

"Insightful! Relevant! Practical! A great tool for any organization trying to implement Sarbanes-Oxley. This guidance is based on actual experiences and proven techniques—it works!"

— Steve Jameson, EVP, Chief Internal Audit & Risk Officer,
Community Trust Bancorp, Inc.

"This document brings together the various compliance and legislative (PCAOB/SEC) issues around the Sarbanes-Oxley legislation. As the act and compliance with it has matured, this document will greatly help practitioners strike the right compliance balance for their organization, whether large or small."

— Roger Herd, General Auditor, Western Refining, Inc.

"This guide is not only useful for those in management who have to deal with internal control over financial reporting for the first time or who encounter major changes in their organization requiring renewed attention. I believe this guide is useful for all, publically trading or not, private and public sector, because it supports accountability and transparency, which have and will always require ultimate attention and effort."

— *Dominique Vincenti, Vice President, Internal Audit, Nordstrom*

"The IIA *Guide for Management By Internal Control Practitioners* is a real action guide that enables its reader to drive a successful Sarbanes-Oxley 404 program."

— *Mathias Braje, Governance, Risk, and Compliance Senior Expert,*
SAP AG

"This is the best Sarbanes-Oxley 404 guide out there for management."

— *Denielle deWynter, Senior Director, The McGraw-Hill Companies*

FOREWORD BY RICHARD M. STEINBERG

As a CEO, chief financial officer (CFO), or other member of corporate management dealing with Sarbanes-Oxley Section 404, you've probably heard more about and spent more time with internal control than you ever imagined—or ever wanted to. Your company likely has incurred significant costs associated with 404, far exceeding what legislators and regulators said they expected. The result was senior management and staff dealing with the assessment and reporting requirements, and boards and audit committees spending more time on monitoring, thereby being diverted from activities viewed as adding more value. With only so many hours in a day, already hard-pressed executives struggled to deal with strategy implementation, leadership responsibilities, major deals, opening or expanding business operations and markets, and tending to myriad business matters requiring their attention. Some companies even exited the public markets, others decided not to go public in the first place, and some foreign companies decided not to use our capital markets, with a potentially adverse effect on capital formation and resulting economic implications.

While the cost has been high, a number of benefits are attributed to Sarbanes-Oxley Section 404. Senior managers and boards of directors became more confident in the reliability of the financial reports on which they sign off, and investors gained increased comfort with information available to the capital markets. Armed with new information about how business processes actually work—often different from the ways those processes were originally designed—management teams identified ways to reduce labor and effort while enhancing process effectiveness. And processes were enhanced to provide not only data but valuable information to make better business decisions. Companies discovered, for example, that within their vast and disparate databases they own information valuable for enhancing marketing, customer service, and other business objectives. A number of companies found that some data they had been using for decision-making was, well, less than reliable. As a result of the 404 process, they enhanced the accuracy, completeness, and relevance of critical data assets for use in making smarter decisions. And some companies used the internal control assessment and enhancement process as a foundation for initiating an enterprise risk management process, though success in that regard has been spotty.

Regardless of whether and how it is valued, Sarbanes-Oxley is here to stay. You have probably been briefed not only on Section 404 but also on Section 302 on disclosure controls and procedures, and the Committee of Sponsoring Organizations of the Treadway Commission's (COSO's) *Internal Control – Integrated Framework*, the U.S. Public Company Accounting Oversight Board's (PCAOB's) Auditing Standard No. 5, the U.S. Securities and Exchange Commission's (SEC's) guidance to management, and your external auditor's guidance materials. And you may have been exposed to earlier editions of *Sarbanes-Oxley Section 404: A Guide for Management by Internal Controls Practitioners*. This guide is directed to CEOs and CFOs who must sign off on the required internal control-related reports and to staff supporting their companies' 404 assessment initiatives—and the good news is that this third edition has been significantly updated. Author Norman Marks brings his years of experience in providing guidance for cost-effective assessments of internal control, weaving practical and experienced-based knowledge and thought leadership into descriptions of authoritative materials. While directed at management, the book also highlights how chief audit executives and their staffs can play a critically important role supporting management's process.

Considerable judgment needs to be brought to bear as you continue to refine your 404 assessment process to enhance effectiveness and efficiency, and gain associated ancillary benefits. Certainly different viewpoints exist across American business regarding interpretations of 404-related regulatory standards and guidance materials. There are and will continue to be differences of opinion among company managements and 404 experts as to what is required in the assessment process and how it is best conducted. Readers of this guide will benefit from Normal Marks' broad-based knowledge and perspective, and his thoughtful consideration of the issues and alternatives.

— Richard M. Steinberg, CEO,

Steinberg Governance Advisors,

former PwC Corporate Governance Practice Leader,

and author of *Governance, Risk Management, and Compliance* (Wiley, 2011)

COSO Principal Contributor

FOREWORD BY DOMINIQUE VINCENTI

ONE MAY THINK that compliance with Section 404 of the Sarbanes-Oxley act is an old story that does not require much attention by now. I would probably be of that opinion, biased by the fact that I have been dealing with organizations that have had to comply from day one. Those organizations have now almost seven years of compliance under their belts, the discipline is now well embedded, the discussion at the audit committee level is healthy, and the appropriate attention is given to the matter by all players—in particular, by management.

But let's not dismiss the relevance of the topic too quickly:

- Initial public offerings (IPOs) have bounced back since becoming nonexistent during the financial crisis. Although much slower than they were in the mid-2000s, the average number of IPOs per month in the United States is about 14 (about 170 per year).

- The mergers and acquisitions market is very active. Cross-border merger activity rose to $96.6 billion for year-to-date 2011, up 59 percent from 2010 and the strongest start for cross-border mergers and acquisitions since 2008. There have been thousands of deals that resulted in dramatically changing business environments and processes for those organizations, and dramatic changes in their control environment over financial reporting.

- Hundreds of new leaders and managers are growing into new jobs every day and find themselves exposed for the first time to this topic.

- The U.S. Public Company Accounting Oversight Board (PCAOB) is constantly revisiting standards and expectations as experience is accumulated and environments change, requiring "veterans" of the matter to stay vigilant and avoid complacency.

I could go on and on, but I think that I made my point. Sarbanes-Oxley Section 404 remains an important topic for management to consider and deal with.

The 2008 financial crisis, the 2011 sovereign debt crisis, and, unfortunately, other crises in the making remind us every day that the global economy is largely tied up in the trust and confidence the investment community places in the economic players.

This book is not only useful for those in management who have to deal with internal control over financial reporting for the first time or who encounter major changes in their organization requiring renewed attention, I believe it is useful for all—publically traded or not, private and public sector—because it supports accountability and transparency, which have and will always require ultimate attention and effort.

— Dominique Vincenti
Vice President, Internal Audit, Nordstrom

Acknowledgments

I would like to thank The IIA—its CEO and staff—for their support throughout the update process. I would also like to express my appreciation for the valuable insights of the following expert practitioners who were kind enough to review drafts and suggest improvements:

- Mathias Braje, Governance, Risk and Compliance Senior Expert, SAP AG

- James DeLoach, Managing Director, Protiviti, Inc.

- Denielle deWynter, Senior Director, The McGraw-Hill Companies

- Robert Hirth, Executive Vice President, Global Internal Audit, Protiviti, Inc.

- Larry Harrington, Vice President, Internal Audit, Raytheon Company

- Roger Herd, General Auditor, Western Refining, Inc.

- Steven E. Jameson, EVP, Chief Internal Audit & Risk Officer, Community Trust Bancorp, Inc.

- James Rose, Vice President and Chief Audit Executive – Fortune 100 Health and Wellness Company; Audit Committee Member – UN Global Disaster Relief Agency

- James Roth, PhD, CIA, CCSA, CRMA, President, AuditTrends LLC

- Rick Steinberg, CEO, Steinberg Governance Advisors

- Dominique Vincenti, Vice President, Internal Audit, Nordstrom

- Rod Winters, General Manager, Finance Operations, Microsoft Corporation

In addition, I offer thanks to the following people who contributed to previous editions of the book:

Bruce Adamec	Roger Herd
Pierre Pradal	James M. Sylph
Heriot Prentice	Steve Jameson
Dick Anderson	Jay Taylor
Larry Rittenberg	Tim Leech
Doug Anderson	Jeffrey Thomson
Peter Schlesiona	Sandford Liebesman
Hubertus Buderath	Louis Vaurs
Kyoko Shimizu	Warren Malmquist
Jackie Cain	Curt Verschoor
Gil Simonetti	Patricia Miller
Lee Ann Campbell	Philip Moulton
Dan Swanson	Jody Whitley

About the Author

Norman Marks, CPA, has been chief audit executive of major global corporations since 1990 and is a recognized thought leader in the profession of internal auditing. He is the author of two of the most downloaded IIA products: this guide and The IIA's Guide to the Assessment of IT Risk (GAIT) Methodology for defining the scope for Sarbanes-Oxley of IT general controls. He is a member of the review boards of several audit and risk management publications (including the magazines of ISACA and The IIA), a frequent speaker internationally, the author of several award-winning articles, and a prolific blogger about internal audit, risk management, governance, and compliance (consistently rating as one of the top influencers in social media on the topics of governance, risk management, and compliance [GRC], internal audit, risk management, and governance).

Marks has been profiled in publications of the American Institute of Certified Public Accountants (AICPA) and The IIA as an innovative and successful internal audit leader. He has been honored as a Fellow of the Open Compliance and Ethics Group for his GRC thought leadership, and as an Honorary Fellow of the Institute of Risk Management for his contributions to risk management.

How to Use This Guide

ORGANIZATIONS CAN USE this guide to ensure their program for assessing the system of internal control over financial reporting is both effective and efficient. They may use it to:

- Rationalize the scope of their program, both to ensure it includes the "right" key controls, but especially to limit the scope and cost of the program to what is necessary to assess the system of internal control over financial reporting.

- Supplement and extend the guidance for management that has been provided by the U.S. Securities and Exchange Commission (SEC).

- Ensure their program reflects the updated 2013 COSO *Internal Control – Integrated Framework.*

- Ensure a consistent understanding across the enterprise of the provisions of Section 404 of the U.S. Sarbanes-Oxley Act of 2002.

- Understand the relationship between Sarbanes-Oxley Sections 302 and 404.

- Design a scope of work for their Sarbanes-Oxley assessment[1] that is top-down and risk-based.

- Understand key controls and how to identify them.

- Appreciate alternative methods, including the use of technology, to test key controls.

- Ensure deficiencies are assessed based on the risk of material misstatement.

- Work effectively with the external auditors.

- Consider the role of internal audit in the Sarbanes-Oxley program.

- Assess and improve the efficiency of their Sarbanes-Oxley program.

- Improve the overall efficiency of their internal control systems, not just the controls relied on for financial reporting.

- Integrate their Sarbanes-Oxley program into the overall enterprisewide risk management program and understand the relationship between the program and governance, risk management, and compliance.

As explained in chapter 2, companies subject to Sarbanes-Oxley-like laws and regulations in other countries can use and benefit from most of the guidance in the guide. Based on their roles in their organizations and responsibilities for Sarbanes-Oxley, readers may use the guide in its entirety or read specific chapters based on interest.

Please note that the author is not a lawyer and this guide should not be considered as legal advice for the purpose of interpreting the laws and regulations discussed here.

INTRODUCTION

MANY ORGANIZATIONS HAVE provided guidance on the subject of the U.S. Sarbanes-Oxley Act of 2002 and management's annual assessment of its system of internal control over financial reporting (ICFR).

- The U.S. Public Company Accounting Oversight Board (PCAOB) provided an updated standard for external auditors in May 2007: AS 5, *An Audit of Internal Control Over Financial Reporting That Is Integrated with an Audit of Financial Statements.*

- Management actions are governed by the U.S. Securities and Exchange Commission (SEC) and not the PCAOB. While the SEC endorsed AS 5, it also provided its own *Commission Guidance Regarding Management's Report on Internal Control Over Financial Reporting Under Section 13(a) or 15(d) of the Securities Exchange Act of 1934* in June 2007. This high-level guidance is not mandatory for management, but following it provides a safe harbor.

- Each of the major certified public accounting (CPA) firms and other providers of audit services have published extensive and valuable guidance, generally consistent with that of the PCAOB and SEC.

- The IT Governance Institute, established by ISACA in 1998, published *IT Control Objectives for Sarbanes-Oxley, 2nd edition,* in 2006. It has not been updated to reflect AS 5 but contains useful guidance that is referenced on occasion in this guide.

As noted above, following the SEC's guidance provides management with a safe harbor. However, the guidance is at a high level and management may find additional, more detailed assistance is required. This document provides that additional level of assistance.

The guide includes frequent references not only to SEC but also to PCAOB guidance because the greater level of detail in the latter is often helpful. In addition, as discussed later, it may be easier to obtain a higher level of external auditor reliance on management's testing if management's and the auditor's approaches are aligned.

In 2013, COSO updated its *Internal Control – Integrated Framework*. The framework is designed to address the system of internal control for all objectives, not just internal control over financial reporting and compliance with the Sarbanes-Oxley Act. The guidance presented here is consistent with that provided by COSO.

This book is not limited in its applicability to the provisions of Sarbanes-Oxley. Other nations have laws and regulations requiring that management assess its internal control over financial reporting. Programs for complying with these Sarbanes-Oxley-like requirements can be optimized using the principles presented here.

Internal auditors have specialized in the assessment of internal controls for decades. They do so as a service to their organization's audit committee and senior management team, and, therefore, have extensive insight into the operation of those controls and the constraints on management in providing those controls. They are experts[1] in the theory and practice of internal controls and related auditing.

This guide—published by The IIA, which is the globally recognized authority and standard-maker for internal auditing—is written for management by experienced internal auditors who have worked on internal controls hand in hand with the board and management. It incorporates and reflects up-to-date guidance from the SEC, the PCAOB, and The IIA, and the real-world experience and insight of practicing internal auditors. Because cost is an issue for all management teams, this guide focuses especially on how total assessment costs, including related external audit fees, can be minimized without impairing the program's effectiveness.

The guide also discusses the interplay between the requirements of Section 404 and those of Section 302. The latter requires annual and quarterly certifications by the CEO and principal financial officer—typically the chief financial officer (CFO)[2]—that include assessments of internal controls.

I encourage readers to review their Sarbanes-Oxley program with the head of their internal audit activity, especially how the program ensures efficiency and minimizes disruption to the business. The internal auditor is uniquely positioned to provide internal consulting on the adequacy of their design and on the entire management assessment and testing process. To this end, this guide contains a checklist in chapter 12 that may be of value in assessing the efficiency of the program.

SUMMARY FOR THE CEO AND CFO

WHEN THE UNITED States Congress passed the U.S. Sarbanes-Oxley Act of 2002, the intent was to drive improvements in companies' internal controls. The benefits were seen as greater assurance to shareholders and other stakeholders in published financial reports. Compliance costs were of lesser significance and underestimated. Arguably, the benefits have been obtained and management has increased the focus on driving down compliance cost.

According to a 2011 study by Ernst & Young, the average company's annual spend for Sarbanes-Oxley compliance is $2,766,742—37 percent spent at least $2 million each year, and 14 percent spent more than $5 million.

However, Ernst & Young also report that only about half of companies performed a rationalization or optimization exercise in the last year. My experience is that many companies can still make significant improvements in their Sarbanes-Oxley program, including realizing important reductions in cost.

This guide will help managers responsible for the Sarbanes-Oxley program to focus on achieving success at the lowest possible cost, including external auditor fees. It provides:

- A clear understanding of the requirements of Sarbanes-Oxley and the fundamentals of internal control.

- Advice on ensuring that the program is consistent with the updated 2013 COSO *Internal Control – Integrated Framework*.

- A discussion of how the annual requirements of Section 404 relate to the quarterly requirements of Section 302 (i.e., the quarterly certification by the CEO and CFO).

- An explanation with practical suggestions for each phase of the program, including areas of difficulty—the identification of key controls, the use of technology, assessing deficiencies, and the final assessment.

- Advice on how to reach a fair assessment that does not mislead investors regarding the condition of internal controls and the reliability of financial statements. I believe management's formal assessment should reflect its belief that the system of internal control provides reasonable assurance of the reliability of *future*[1] financial statements[2] and that reliability is based on the likelihood of an error that would be material to a reasonable investor. In addition, an assessment that controls are not effective simply because there has been a restatement of previously issued financial statements may mislead the investor regarding the current state of internal controls and reliability of future financial statements.

- A checklist to help management assess the efficiency of its program.

- Thoughts on improving the overall design of controls.

- How to work collaboratively with the external auditor and why it is important.

- Advice on the role of the internal auditor.

- How to integrate the Sarbanes-Oxley and ERM programs, and the relationship with governance, risk management, and compliance.

Some companies adopted a methodology for Sarbanes-Oxley that is rules-based,[3] which can lead to an assessment that is neither effective nor efficient. Instead, management should use judgment to develop and operate a continuing Sarbanes-Oxley program that is principles-based. Executives should understand that:

- Management has a great deal of flexibility in designing and implementing its Sarbanes-Oxley program, much more than is available to the external auditor.[4]

- Both management and the external auditor have been encouraged by the U.S. Securities and Exchange Commission (SEC) and the U.S. Public Company Accounting Oversight Board (PCAOB) to use their judgment and develop an approach that is top-down and risk-based. The Sarbanes-Oxley program should include coverage of all areas where the inherent risk (i.e., the risk before the quality of internal controls is considered) of an error or fraud that could lead to a material misstatement[5] is at least reasonably possible.[6] There is no need for the program to assess and test every control related to financial reporting, even those that might be considered significant deficiencies if they failed (see the definition of "significant deficiency" provided later in this guide).

■ Every organization is required[7] to use a recognized internal controls framework for its Sarbanes-Oxley program. The only framework recognized by the SEC is COSO's *Internal Control – Integrated Framework*. The 2013 update spells out the requirements for effective internal control, including guidance that management should use its judgment both in designing and assessing internal control over financial reporting. It asserts that effective internal control is achieved when (a) it "reduces, to an acceptable level, the risk of not achieving an objective (translated for Sarbanes-Oxley, this means that it provides reasonable assurance that the risk of a material omission or error in the financial statements filed with the SEC is low), and (b) relevant principles of internal control (as detailed in the framework) are present and functioning. Management should use its judgment, based on the level of risk, in setting the level and nature of work required to confirm that the principles are present and functioning."

> **KEY POINT:**
> **MANAGEMENT'S ROLE**
>
> Management has a great deal of flexibility in designing and implementing its Section 404 program, much more than is available to the external auditor.

On May 16, 2005, the SEC staff issued *Statement on Management's Report on Internal Control over Financial Reporting* that said (emphasis added):

"An overall purpose of internal control over financial reporting is to foster the preparation of reliable financial statements. Reliable financial statements must be materially accurate. Therefore, a central purpose of the assessment of internal control over financial reporting is to identify material weaknesses that have, as indicated by their very definition, more than a remote likelihood of leading to a material misstatement in the financial statements. While identifying control deficiencies and significant deficiencies represents an important component of management's assessment, *the overall focus of internal control reporting should be on those items that could result in material errors in the financial statements.*

"In adopting its rules implementing Section 404, the Commission expressly declined to prescribe the scope of assessment or the amount of testing and documentation required by management. *The scope and process of the assessment should be reasonable, and the assessment (including testing) should be supported by a reasonable level of evidential matter.*

"*Each company should also use informed judgment in documenting and testing its controls to fit its own operations, risks, and procedures. Management should use its own experience and informed judgment in designing an assessment process that fits the needs of that company. Management should not allow the goal and purpose of the internal control over financial reporting provisions—the production of reliable financial statements—to be overshadowed by the process.*"

Similarly, AS 5[8] directs the external auditor to focus on the risk of material errors:

"The auditor's objective in an audit of internal control over financial reporting is to express an opinion on the effectiveness of the company's internal control over financial reporting. Because a company's internal control cannot be considered effective if one or more material weaknesses exist, to form a basis for expressing an opinion, the auditor must plan and perform the audit to obtain competent evidence that is sufficient to obtain reasonable assurance about whether material weaknesses exist as of the date specified in management's assessment."

KEY POINTS:
SEC STATEMENT

► "The overall focus of internal control reporting should be on those items that could result in material errors in the financial statements."

► "Management should not allow the goal and purpose of the internal control over financial reporting provisions—the production of reliable financial statements—to be overshadowed by the process."

In 2007, the PCAOB released a report on their inspections of external auditors' work on internal controls over financial reporting[9] that is still relevant. Their findings included:

"...evidence that most firms had made progress in integrating their audits (for example, by using the same engagement team to perform both the financial statement audit and the audit of internal control over financial reporting). The inspectors also observed more instances in which auditors approached the audit of internal control from the top down and thus did a better job of focusing their testing and evaluation on the relevant company-level controls. As a result, they spent less time testing a larger number of controls that existed at the process, transaction, and application levels. Several of the firms achieved greater efficiencies by varying the extent of their testing commensurate with the level of risk and, generally, auditors used the work of others more in the second year of implementing AS No. 2 than in the first year."

> **KEY POINTS:**
> PCAOB FINDINGS
>
> ► Some auditors did not fully integrate their audits.
>
> ► Some auditors failed to apply a top-down approach to testing controls.

"In each of the four areas on which the inspection teams focused, the reviews identified ways in which auditors could have been more efficient. While these observations varied in form and degree among the firms and engagement teams, the lessons learned can benefit auditors generally. The most common observations were:

- Some auditors did not fully integrate their audits.

- Some auditors failed to apply a top-down approach to testing controls.

- Some auditors assessed the level of risk only at the account level and not at the assertion level. As a result, those auditors likely expended more effort than necessary when testing controls for assertions that were lower risk. In a few cases, auditors tested the same controls that the issuer had tested, without assessing whether this was necessary to sufficiently address the risk that a relevant assertion might be misstated.

- Some auditors could have increased their use of the work of others."

Companies continue to report that their auditors have not adopted the top-down and risk-based approach mandated by AS 5, often because they had material weaknesses in the past. They say that the auditors want to see the weaknesses corrected before cutting the scope of work; however, external auditors who use this approach are not complying with mandated auditing standards, and management should press them to change.

Executives should also understand that:

- Management is *not* required to adopt the same methodology as the external auditors, although there may be advantages in using a similar approach. AS 5 is mandatory for external auditors, but not for management. However, management should give strong consideration to following the approach described in AS 5. One of the greatest sources of cost savings is derived from maximizing the degree of reliance placed by the external auditors on management testing. When management and auditors use the same language and a consistent approach, reliance is easier to achieve.

- Management may elect to follow a different methodology than the external auditors. If it does, management and the auditor should review and reconcile the results of their two approaches. If the external auditors identify key controls to test that are not included in management's scope, management may decide to add them. Even though management has determined they are not necessary, adding them to the scope might enable the external auditors to limit their independent testing and reduce the company's total compliance cost.

- The regulators believed the greatest benefit from Section 404 was that it would provide greater assurance to investors and others that they could rely on management's published financials. Arguably, the value of that assurance extends beyond the current set of financial statements (to which the Section 404 assessment is attached) as they are subject to a separate assertion by management and opinion by the external auditors on their adequacy. The added value is in providing comfort with respect to the reliability of financial statements that will be published in the *future*. The Section 404 assessment indicates to the investor whether the system of internal control is sufficiently robust such that the risk of material error in *future* financial statements is remote or less.[10]

In hindsight, perhaps the greatest value has been a clear improvement in companies' systems of internal control over financial reporting. Protiviti[11] reported that 45 percent of companies believe their internal controls improved in 2011 compared to 2010. Two-thirds believed that the benefits outweighed the costs.

In practical terms, management's assessment of the system of internal control over financial reporting should reflect whether it believes the risk of material misstatements in financial statements filed with the SEC over the next 12 months[12] is less than reasonably likely. An alternative view is whether management believes its system of internal control over financial reporting contains any material weaknesses, representing a reasonable possibility that financial statements filed with the SEC over the next 12 months will contain material errors.

As companies adopt the 2013 update of COSO's *Internal Control – Integrated Framework*, it should recognize the need to formally assess whether the principles are present and functioning (i.e., achieved). I recommend that management perform a self-assessment (as described below) and

> **KEY POINT:**
> COST MANAGEMENT
>
> ► Use a top-down, risk-based approach to limit the number of key controls.
>
> ► Maximize reliance by the external auditor on management testing.
>
> ► Execute controls flawlessly.

have provided guidance for each principle in this book. The level of work that is performed, including the identification and testing of related key controls, should be based on management's judgment of the level of risk. (See detailed discussion below.)

One of the greatest areas of cost savings over the last few years has been the reduction of external costs (i.e., costs other than internal employees' time). While some companies continue to make significant use of third-party providers of consulting and audit services to perform testing and sometimes manage their Sarbanes-Oxley program, most have reduced costs by hiring project managers and testing personnel.

External audit fees related to Sarbanes-Oxley work remain significant, but many companies have seen reductions[13] as auditors moved to a top-down, risk-based approach and increased reliance on management's work.

Management can continue to contain and even reduce costs with a focus on these areas:

- **Reducing the number of key controls (i.e., the controls that have to be tested) through a top-down, risk-based approach** that focuses on controls that will prevent or detect material errors. Companies and external auditors have historically tested controls that are not key under this definition, adding unnecessary work and cost. Controls that are not likely to result in material error should not be considered "key" and do not need to be within management's scope for Sarbanes-Oxley.

  From time to time, the question is asked as to how many key controls "best practice" companies have identified and are testing. (Alternatively, the question is "How many key controls should I have?") There is no such "ideal" number of key controls. Best practice is to define the key controls required to manage the risk of a material error in the financial statements for your organization. The number will depend on factors such as the level of standardized and centralized processes and systems, the level of profit margins (the lower the level, the more potential for errors to be material), and the ability to rely on entity-level controls. This process for selecting key controls is discussed in chapter 7.

- **Using the top-down approach to identify direct entity-level controls** (e.g., month-to-month payroll variance analyses performed during the period-end close process) that provide reasonable assurance that a material misstatement due to a failure in controls within the business process (e.g., within payroll) would be detected. In this situation, it may be possible to remove any business process controls from the scope of work.

- **Maximizing reliance by the external auditors on management testing.** This requires ensuring that management testing is performed by skilled, experienced individuals who are independent of the activity being tested. Many companies use their internal audit activity to perform the testing, because this is the most likely approach to maximize external auditor reliance. (See chapter 15 for a discussion of considerations in the use of internal auditors in the Sarbanes-Oxley program.) Some use other internal staff to perform management testing and may rely on internal audit to review and test their work to ensure it is to appropriate standards.

- **Executing controls flawlessly.** The tolerance level for defects in testing is very low. If the external auditors find even one error in their testing of a control, they may assess the control as not operating effectively. This will require remediation and retesting, potentially doubling the work and adding cost.

- **Documenting the processes and controls clearly and in detail** and ensuring the documentation is updated promptly as processes change.

- **Considering the potential impact on the Sarbanes-Oxley program of process, organization, and system changes during the change process.** Retrofitting controls after the change has been made brings more risk and, in all likelihood, more cost to the program. In fact, changes to processes and systems should include, as requirements, improvements in the level of automated controls and the ability to detect potential errors promptly.

- **Improving the use of technology** to manage the Sarbanes-Oxley program and test key controls. This is discussed in more detail in chapter 11.

- **Completing a substantial portion of management's work, including testing all key controls (even if only limited in sample size) by midyear.** This enables the external auditors to start their work early, which helps with resource scheduling and reduces the risk of finding deficiencies late. In addition, control defects can be detected earlier, with time for remediation and re-testing of the affected controls.

- **Coordinating the various compliance programs** within the company to avoid duplication of effort, and so forth. (See chapter 16 on GRC and Sarbanes-Oxley.)

The above actions will also reduce management and employees' time maintaining documentation, assisting those performing the testing, and so forth.

In the past, most CEOs and chief financial officers (CFOs) have signed their annual and quarterly certifications—which are included in the financial statements filed with the SEC on Form 10-Q and required by Section 302 of Sarbanes-Oxley—without a rigorous examination of internal controls. Ideally, management has integrated the quarterly and annual assessment processes. Although management is not required to test all its key controls every quarter, it should perform some degree of testing each quarter to support the quarterly Section 302 certification.[14] At a minimum, the Section 302 certification process should include a consideration of the status of the Sarbanes-Oxley project, the results of testing, the severity of any identified control deficiencies, and management's corrective action plans. The last section of this guide suggests how management can continue to assess and improve the Sarbanes-Oxley program annually.

It is important for CEOs and CFOs to understand that, while it is important to have effective controls for financial reporting, it is critical to have effective controls to run the business. Controls over the quality and reliability of information used in decision-making, the pricing of sales to customers, or compliance with other laws and regulations are at least as important. As discussed in chapter 15, the internal audit activity can be of significant value, providing assurance over the organization's governance, risk management, and related control processes.

Finally, executives should understand the potential impact of the new technology that is changing the way in which businesses operate. The more significant examples are the move of platforms and applications to the "cloud" and the rapid adoption of smart phones and tablets—mobile devices. This is discussed in more detail in a later section, but the key is to realize that the technology may change the business processes, the nature of risks, and the location of key controls. However, the principles discussed in this guide remain appropriate. The same process should be followed to understand the risks and identify the key controls to test.

Section 404: Rules or Principles

Section 404 required the SEC to develop and publish rules for a management assessment of internal control over financial reporting (ICFR). These rules were completed in June 2003 and updated in June 2007. Changes included removing the requirement for the external auditors to assess management's process for assessing the system of ICFR and revising the definitions of significant deficiency and material weakness. The PCAOB released AS 2, which was approved by the SEC in June 2004 and replaced in May 2007 by AS 5. The SEC rules and PCAOB standard require that:

    a. Management perform a formal assessment of its controls over financial reporting (definition below), including tests that confirm the design and operating effectiveness of the controls.

    b. Management include in its annual report on Form 10-K[1] an assessment of ICFR.

    c. The external auditors provide two opinions as part of a single integrated audit:

        1. An independent opinion on the effectiveness of the system of ICFR.

        2. The traditional opinion on the financial statements.

The SEC rules are worth reviewing carefully. They "require a company's annual report to include an internal control report of management that contains:

- A statement of management's responsibility for establishing and maintaining adequate internal control over financial reporting for the company.

- A statement identifying the framework used by management to conduct the required evaluation of the effectiveness of the company's internal control over financial reporting.

- Management's assessment of the effectiveness of the company's internal control over financial reporting as of the end of the company's most recent fiscal year, including a statement as to whether the company's internal control over financial reporting is effective. The assessment must include disclosure of any "material weaknesses" in the company's internal control over financial reporting. Management is not permitted to conclude that the company's internal control over financial reporting is effective if there are one or more material weaknesses in the company's internal control over financial reporting.

- A statement that the registered public accounting firm that audited the financial statements included in the annual report has issued an attestation report on management's assessment of the registrant's internal control over financial reporting."

The "final rules also require a company to file, as part of the company's annual report, the attestation report of the registered public accounting firm that audited the company's financial statements."

Taking each point in turn:

1. Management is responsible for the system of internal control. This is an important clarification because some management teams had believed[2] the system of internal control was the responsibility of the internal auditor, external auditor, or the CFO. By contrast, an effective system of internal control is the responsibility not just of the CFO but the CEO and the senior executive team as a whole.

2. The assessment must be made using a recognized internal controls framework. Almost all U.S. and global companies have used the Committee of Sponsoring Organizations of the Treadway Commission's (COSO's) *Internal Control – Integrated Framework*,[3] although some have used the Control Objectives for Information and related Technology (COBIT) framework as a supplement to COSO for IT controls. (Both COSO and COBIT are discussed in chapter 3.)

3. The assessment is annual and as of year-end. The SEC has restricted how management can make its assessment, as noted above.

4. The external auditors must perform specified work in relation to management's assessment. The SEC mandated "an attestation report." The PCAOB has interpreted that in AS 5, with SEC consent, to be an independent assessment and formal opinion on the adequacy of the system of internal control over financial reporting.

While the PCAOB has provided detailed—and principles-based—guidance in AS 5 for external auditors, AS 5 is not binding on management. In fact, management has a great deal of flexibility in implementing its Section 404 program. The guidance from the SEC is also principles-based and at a fairly high level.

Management needs to understand AS 5 because it explains how the external auditors will review and evaluate management's assessment process. It is also important if management is going to minimize audit fees by maximizing reliance by the auditors on management testing.

However, management also needs to ensure its process is faithful to the *principles* behind Section 404—that it provides a fair assessment of its internal controls as of its year-end, reflecting whether the system provides reasonable assurance that material misstatements will be prevented or detected.

The following chapters provide a road map for understanding the principles and requirements for Section 404 and implementing an efficient and effective Sarbanes-Oxley program. Chapter 4 explains the requirements of Section 302 (i.e., the quarterly certification by the CEO and CFO of the interim financials) and its relationship with Section 404.

International Versions of Sarbanes-Oxley

A. Background

A number of nations have passed laws and regulations requiring companies to assess and report on their internal controls over financial reporting. These include:

- **China:** State-owned companies and those listed on either the Shanghai or Shenzhen exchanges have to comply (starting in 2012) with the Basic Standard for Internal Control. This is frequently referred to as C-SOX. (Other Chinese companies are encouraged to comply, and Chinese companies listed overseas are required to comply with the Basic Standard in addition to any requirements of the listing exchange.) The regulation requires management to implement effective internal control, self-assess the adequacy of the controls, publish an annual evaluation, and engage third-party auditors to validate the assessment. While this guide focuses only on internal control over financial reporting and the Chinese regulations have a broader view of internal control, the principles in this guide (e.g., the use of a risk-based approach and the identification of key controls) might be of use beyond financial reporting.

- **South Africa:** The King III code requires that companies listed on the Johannesburg Stock Exchange include statements from the board and the audit committee on the effectiveness of internal control over financial reporting in the integrated report. Companies must perform a formally documented review of the system of internal control but are not required to obtain a third-party audit of the controls or management's assessment.

- **Japan:** The Financial Instruments and Exchange Law (often referred to as J-SOX) requires listed companies to assess and provide an assessment of its internal control over financial reporting. They must also engage a third-party auditor to provide an opinion on management's assessment.

- **Canada:** Companies that have listed equity securities are subject to the requirements of Bill 198 (Ontario) as defined in its enabling Multilateral Instrument 52-109 "Certification of Disclosure in Issuers' Annual and Interim Filings." (This is also sometimes referred to as C-SOX—not to be confused with C-SOX in China). The company's CEO and CFO must certify to the effectiveness both of disclosure controls and internal control over financial reporting in a form very similar to that required by Sarbanes-Oxley Section 302. No external auditor assessment of management's certification is required.

- **France:** La Loi de Sécurité Financière, which translates as The French Security Law (also referred to as LSF or Loi Mer), requires that the president of the board of directors or the CEO prepare, in addition to the board's annual management report, a report on the system of internal control, including (for listed companies) an evaluation of the internal control procedures. This report is not limited to internal control over financial reporting. The statutory auditor is required to prepare a report (in addition to the report on the financial statements) presenting its comments on the system of internal control as it relates to the preparation of the financial statements. The Autorité des Marchés Financiers (AMF) has provided a reference framework[1] that is a useful guide for companies seeking to comply with French requirements and implement effective risk management and internal control systems. The reference framework is not binding.

Other countries, such as the United Kingdom and the Netherlands, have laws and regulations requiring listed companies to comply or explain noncompliance with governance codes. These codes typically require management to maintain effective systems of internal control over financial reporting. The Netherlands goes a little further, encouraging (but not mandating) that companies provide a statement acknowledging their responsibility for internal control and their assessment of its condition.

B. USE OF THIS GUIDE

While this guide focuses on Sarbanes-Oxley and its requirements, most of the guidance is relevant and should be of value to management assessments of internal control over financial reporting under other laws and regulations.

The first step is to identify the differences between those other laws and regulations. For example, the role of the external auditor is quite different in Japan, where the auditor is only required to provide an opinion on management's assessment; and in Canada and South Africa, the company is not required to obtain a third-party assessment at all. Management can then design a financial controls assessment process that is appropriate to its specific regulatory environment.

Finally, those chapters of this guide that might be useful can be identified. For example, the following chapters are always likely to be useful:

Chapter 5: Who Is Responsible for Internal Controls?

Chapter 7: Defining the Detailed Scope for Sarbanes-Oxley

Chapter 8: Testing Key Controls

Chapter 9: Assessing the Adequacy of Controls, Including Assessing Deficiencies

Chapter 10: Management's Report on Internal Controls: The End Product

Chapter 11: Using Technology in the Sarbanes-Oxley Program

Chapter 12: Assessing the Efficiency of the Sarbanes-Oxley Program

Chapter 13: An Efficient System of Internal Control Over Financial Reporting

Chapter 15: The Role of Internal Audit

Chapter 16: The Relationship Between Governance, Risk Management, and Compliance; ERM; and Sarbanes-Oxley

Chapter 17: Continuous Improvement

REVISITING THE PRINCIPLES OF INTERNAL CONTROL

A. INTERNAL CONTROL AND ITS LIMITATIONS

There are a number of different definitions for the term *internal control*. For the purposes of Sarbanes-Oxley, the great majority of companies and all the CPA firms[1] use the definition in COSO's *Internal Control – Integrated Framework*. COSO's definition relates to all aspects of internal control, not just that over financial reporting. The following is from the report's executive summary (2013 edition):

"Internal control is a process, effected by an entity's board of directors, management, and other personnel, designed to provide reasonable assurance regarding the achievement of objectives relating to operations, reporting, and compliance."

COSO also says that "internal control is:

- Geared to the achievement of objectives in one or more separate but overlapping categories—operations, reporting, and compliance.

- A process consisting of ongoing tasks and activities—a means to an end, not an end in itself.

- Effected by people—not merely about policy and procedure manuals, systems, and forms, but

> **KEY POINTS:**
> COSO PRINCIPLES OF INTERNAL CONTROL
>
> ► "Internal control is a process, effected by an entity's board of directors, management, and other personnel, designed to provide reasonable assurance regarding the achievement of objectives relating to operations, reporting, and compliance."
>
> ► "While internal control is a process, its effectiveness is a state or condition of the process at one or more points in time."

about people and the actions they take at every level of an organization to affect internal control.

- Able to provide reasonable assurance—but not absolute assurance, to an entity's senior management and board of directors.

- Adaptable to the entity structure—flexible in application for the entire entity or for a particular subsidiary, division, operating unit, or business process."

The 2013 internal control framework provides two key points relating to the assessment of internal control.

- First, it states that "An effective system provides reasonable assurance regarding achievement of an entity's objectives. An effective system of internal control reduces, to an acceptable level, the risk of not achieving an entity objective and may relate to one, two, or all three categories of objectives."

COSO has made public statements that support the application of a top-down and risk-based approach to assessing internal control over financial reporting described in this book and in both SEC and PCAOB guidance.

- COSO continues by explaining requirements for achieving reasonable assurance; these are based on the presence and functioning of five components of internal control and 17 principles. This is discussed in the next section, which is focused on COSO's internal control framework.

The PCAOB, together with the SEC, is responsible for the rules governing the roles and actions of the CPA firms. In AS 5, *An Audit of Internal Control Over Financial Reporting Performed in Conjunction with an Audit of Financial Statements*, the PCAOB has a definition that is consistent with that of COSO, although limited to financial reporting. It is also consistent in all material respects with the definition used by the SEC.[2] They define ICFR as:

"A process designed by, or under the supervision of, the company's principal executive and principal financial officers, or persons performing similar functions, and effected by the company's board of directors, management, and other personnel, to provide reasonable assurance regarding the reliability of financial reporting and the preparation of financial statements for external purposes in accordance with generally accepted accounting principles and includes those policies and procedures that:

1. Pertain to the maintenance of records that, in reasonable detail, accurately and fairly reflect the transactions and dispositions of the assets of the company;

2. Provide reasonable assurance that transactions are recorded as necessary to permit preparation of financial statements in accordance with generally accepted accounting principles, and that receipts and expenditures of the company are being made only in accordance with authorizations of management and directors of the company; and

3. Provide reasonable assurance regarding prevention or timely detection of unauthorized acquisition, use, or disposition of the company's assets that could have a material effect on the financial statements."

There are several key points in these definitions:

1. Internal control is a *process*. However, any assessment of its effectiveness is made at a point in time. Management must assess the adequacy of its ICFR as of year-end, even though the system operates continuously—not only all year but over multiple years. Management also needs to be aware, though, that an assessment as of a point in time is likely to be interpreted by investors and others as indicative of its continuing effectiveness. Stakeholders are concerned with whether the internal controls are sufficient to provide comfort, not only with respect to the reliability of the current set of financial statements but also of future financial statements.

> **KEY POINT:**
> **REASONABLE ASSURANCE**
>
> "An internal control system, no matter how well conceived and operated, can provide only reasonable—not absolute—assurance to management and the board regarding achievement of an entity's objectives. The likelihood of achievement is affected by limitations inherent in all internal control systems. These include the realities that judgments in decision-making can be faulty, and that breakdowns can occur because of simple error or mistake."

2. Internal control only provides *reasonable assurance*. COSO's executive summary expands on this point:

"An effective system of internal control provides management and the board of directors with reasonable assurance regarding achievement of an entity's objectives. The term "reasonable assurance" rather than "absolute assurance" acknowledges that limitations exist in all systems of internal control, and that uncertainties and risks may exist, which no one can confidently predict with precision. Absolute assurance is not possible.

"Reasonable assurance does not imply that an entity will always achieve its objectives. Effective internal control increases the likelihood of an entity achieving its objectives. However, the likelihood of achievement is affected by limitations inherent in all systems of internal control, such as human error, the uncertainty inherent in judgment, and the potential impact of external events outside management's control. Additionally, a system of internal control can be circumvented if people collude. Further, if management is able to override controls, the entire system may fail. Even though an entity's system of internal control should be designed to prevent and detect collusion, human error, and management override, an effective system of internal control can experience a failure."

In its guidance for management, the SEC states (*emphasis* added):

"The 'reasonable assurance' referred to in the Commission's implementing rules relates to similar language in the Foreign Corrupt Practices Act of 1977 (FCPA). Exchange Act Section 13(b)(7) defines 'reasonable assurance' and 'reasonable detail' as *such level of detail and degree of assurance as would satisfy prudent officials in the conduct of their own affairs.*" The Commission has long held that "reasonableness" is not an "absolute standard of exactitude for corporate records." In addition, the Commission recognizes that while "reasonableness" is an objective standard, there is a range of judgments that an issuer might make as to what is "reasonable" in implementing Section 404 and the Commission's rules. Thus, the terms "reasonable," "reasonably," and "reasonableness" in the context of Section 404 implementation do not imply a single conclusion or methodology but encompass the full range of appropriate potential conduct, conclusions, or methodologies upon which an issuer may reasonably base its decisions."

An effective system of internal control can only provide this *reasonable assurance.* When assessing its adequacy, management needs to determine whether errors—even if they resulted in a material error in the financial statements—are the result of a "simple error or mistake" that is a momentary or one-time failure, rather than an indication that the system no longer provides *reasonable assurance* that a material error in the financials will not be prevented or detected. COSO, the PCAOB, and the SEC refer to the concept of a prudent official or reasonable person's view, which should be considered when determining whether the system of internal control provides reasonable assurance.

The PCAOB states that *reasonable* is a "high level of assurance." It refers to the "understanding that there is a *remote likelihood* [emphasis added] that material misstatements will not be prevented or detected on a timely basis." This is fully consistent with the way in which management and the external auditors should assess the overall system of internal control. As noted later, the external auditors typically use a range of 5 percent to 10 percent for remote likelihood.

The SEC has not provided a specific standard with which the effectiveness of internal control should be measured. Instead, in the words of their commentary on the final rules, they have set a "threshold for concluding that a company's internal control over financial reporting is effective." That threshold is the presence of one or more material weaknesses. Therefore, management can assess ICFR as effective if there are no control deficiencies such that a material error is reasonably possible.

> **KEY POINT:**
> **EFFECTIVE INTERNAL CONTROL OVER FINANCIAL REPORTING**
>
> Management can assess ICFR as effective if there are no material weaknesses

Stating the issue more simply, a system of internal control provides a reasonable level of assurance with respect to filed financial statements (i.e., for Sarbanes-Oxley) when:

- The cumulative risk of a material misstatement due to known control weakness is not reasonably possible (i.e., the likelihood is 5 percent or less).[3]

- Any control weaknesses identified by management and external or internal auditors are corrected promptly.

- The management team believes the level of controls is appropriate to the organization, enabling the publishing of reliable financial statements for external use (i.e., SEC filings).

3. Internal control over the integrity of a company's financial statements is part of the overall system of internal control. In practice, there can be significant overlap between controls designed to provide assurance over the financials and those that provide assurance relative to operational effectiveness or compliance. For example, monitoring the cost of units sold is an important control for both financial reporting and for ensuring the efficiency and effectiveness of operations. When assessing control deficiencies to determine the need and value of enhancing controls, management should consider the risk not only to the financial statements but also to the efficiency of operations or compliance with applicable rules and regulations.

4. Another point of significance is that for Sarbanes-Oxley purposes, ICFR only addresses the controls providing assurance over financial statements filed with the SEC. It does not necessarily address controls over:

    - Other financial statements, including those provided as part of statutory reporting to foreign governments or to financial institutions as may be required by debt instruments.

    - Financial reports used in internal management's decision-making (e.g., monthly management metrics).

    - Other sections of the 10-K, such as Management's Discussion and Analysis (MD&A).

    - Earnings releases and proxy statements.

Clearly, management needs to have effective controls over all forms of financial reporting and may consider either extending its own assessment to cover these areas or asking its internal audit activity to perform procedures relative to these areas.

B. THE COSO INTERNAL CONTROL FRAMEWORK

Management is required to assess its system of ICFR using a recognized framework. Most have selected COSO's *Internal Control – Integrated Framework*, which has been recognized as appropriate by the SEC and PCAOB.

COSO's internal control framework describes internal controls as consisting of five interrelated components that are described by COSO as:

- **Control Environment.** "The control environment is the set of standards, processes, and structures that provide the basis for carrying out internal control across the organization. The board of directors and senior management establish the tone at the top regarding the importance of internal control and expected standards of conduct."

- **Risk Assessment.** "Risk assessment involves a dynamic and iterative process for identifying and analyzing risks to achieving the entity's objectives, forming a basis for determining how risks should be managed. Management considers possible changes in the external environment and within its own business model that may impede its ability to achieve its objectives."

- **Control Activities.** "Control activities are the actions established by policies and procedures to help ensure that management directives to mitigate risks to the achievement of objectives are carried out. Control activities are performed at all levels of the entity and at various stages within business processes, and over the technology environment."

- **Information and Communication.** "Information is necessary for the entity to carry out internal control responsibilities in support of achievement of its objectives. Communication occurs both internally and externally and provides the organization with the information needed to carry out day-to-day controls. Communication enables personnel to understand internal control responsibilities and their importance to the achievement of objectives."

- **Monitoring.** "Ongoing evaluations, separate evaluations, or some combination of the two are used to ascertain whether each of the five components of internal control, including controls to effect the principles within each component, is present and functioning. Findings are evaluated and deficiencies are communicated in a timely manner, with serious matters reported to senior management and to the board."

The system of internal control includes activities (i.e., controls) in each of these components. The controls operate at two or (generally) more levels within the organization:

- **Entity-Level** activities generally operate at a corporate level, and typical examples are corporate policies, the activities of the board of directors, and the period-ending financial close.

- The **Activity Level** generally relates to individual business locations or business processes. Examples might include accounts payable, direct supervision of employees, and the hiring process for new employees.

- Controls may also operate at an **Intermediate Level**. For example, in a global organization controls may operate within corporate financial reporting (entity-level), the division and/or regional controller's team (intermediate level), and the local plant's accounting function (activity-level).

Most of the controls that are assessed are located at the activity level. However, particular attention to entity and intermediate-level controls is required because:

- These controls are presumed to have a pervasive effect on the activities of the entire company, or a substantial portion of it.

- Many of the control deficiencies underlying the more public accounting issues of the last several years, including Enron and WorldCom, were at the entity level (e.g., tone at the top).

- Assessing entity and intermediate-level controls early, if not first, can often affect the selection of controls to be tested at the activity level. For example, a review of month-to-month fluctuations in payroll costs that is performed as part of the financial period-end close may be sufficient in some companies to detect material errors arising from payroll processing. In that case, management may decide there is no need to perform additional testing within the payroll process itself.

Activities in each of the five components can be found at any level. For example:

- *Control Environment* activities include the organization's code of conduct (an entity-level control) and employee candidate background checks (performed at the activity level).

- *Risk Assessment* includes assessing the risk of an unassertive audit committee (entity level) or the existence of excess inventory (managed at the division, or intermediate level).

- *Control Activities* include top-level reviews performed as part of the corporate close process (entity level) and bank reconciliations (activity level).

- *Information and Communication* includes information on warranty claims used to calculate the warranty reserve as part of the financial close process (entity level), and communicating to employees performance expectations (activity level).

> **KEY POINT:**
> COSO ACTIVITIES
>
> Activities in each of the five [COSO] components can be found at any level.

- *Monitoring* includes the internal audit activity (entity level) and the direct supervision of payroll staff and review of their account reconciliations (activity level).

The COSO framework has identified 17 principles, which it describes as "fundamental concepts associated with components." They are organized in the framework by component:

Control Environment

1. The organization demonstrates a commitment to integrity and ethical values.

2. The board of directors demonstrates independence from management and exercises oversight of the development and performance of internal control.

3. Management establishes, with board oversight, structures, reporting lines, and appropriate authorities and responsibilities in the pursuit of objectives.

4. The organization demonstrates a commitment to attract, develop, and retain competent individuals in alignment with objectives.

5. The organization holds individuals accountable for their internal control responsibilities in the pursuit of objectives.

Risk Assessment

6. The organization specifies objectives with sufficient clarity to enable the identification and assessment of risks relating to objectives.

7. The organization identifies risks to the achievement of its objectives across the entity and analyzes risks as a basis for determining how the risks should be managed.

8. The organization considers the potential for fraud in assessing risks to the achievement of objectives.

9. The organization identifies and assesses changes that could significantly impact the system of internal control.

Control Activities

10. The organization selects and develops control activities that contribute to the mitigation of risks to the achievement of objectives to acceptable levels.

11. The organization selects and develops general control activities over technology to support the achievement of objectives.

12. The organization deploys control activities through policies that establish what is expected and procedures that put policies into action.

Information and Communication

13. The organization obtains or generates and uses relevant, quality information to support the functioning of internal control.

14. The organization internally communicates information, including objectives and responsibilities for internal control, necessary to support the functioning of internal control.

15. The organization communicates with external parties regarding matters affecting the functioning of internal control.

Monitoring Activities

16. The organization selects, develops, and performs ongoing and/or separate evaluations to ascertain whether the components of internal control are present and functioning.

17. The organization evaluates and communicates internal control deficiencies in a timely manner to those parties responsible for taking corrective action, including senior management and the board of directors, as appropriate.

COSO asserts that effective internal control requires that all *relevant* principles are present and functioning (i.e., achieved). While an argument could be made that some of these principles are not relevant to internal control over financial reporting, that is a difficult position to maintain. I recommend that management consider all 17 principles to be relevant but vary the level of work performed (i.e., the number of key controls identified and the level of testing performed on each) based on risk. This is discussed further below.

A number of companies use a separate framework to supplement COSO when assessing IT controls. COBIT[4] was developed by the Information Systems Audit and Control Association's IT Governance Institute in 1994 and is widely used by IT audit professionals in the United States and overseas. Organizations should note that the SEC has not recognized COBIT as a framework for internal control over financial reporting for Sarbanes-Oxley, but has accepted its use to supplement COSO with respect to IT-related controls.

COSO published *Internal Control Over Financial Reporting – Guidance for Smaller Public Companies* in 2006. This three-volume publication[5] includes useful information on the application of COSO's internal control framework to Sarbanes-Oxley. Although it is targeted at smaller public companies, it may be useful to management of companies of any size.

Additional information on internal controls may be obtained from the head of the internal audit activity, The IIA, or the external auditors.

Chapter 4

What Constitutes an Effective System of Internal Control as It Relates to the Requirements of Section 404?

MANAGEMENT NEEDS TO determine whether the system of internal control in effect as of the date of the assessment provides reasonable assurance that material errors, in either interim or annual financial statements, will be prevented or detected.

Management is able to make this assessment by:

1. Identifying, assessing, and testing the design and operating effectiveness of the key controls that will either prevent or detect material errors from transactions in significant accounts in the financial statements, or in the way the financial statements are prepared and presented.

2. Assessing whether any control deficiencies identified in the above process represent, either individually or in aggregate, a reasonable possibility of a material error (i.e., a material weakness).

If the scope and quality of management's identification, assessment, and testing of key controls is sufficient to address all major risks to the integrity of the financial statements and no material weaknesses are identified, then management will normally be able to assess the system of ICFR as effective.

However, the presence of a single material weakness precludes management from making such an assessment. This is appropriate, as a material weakness by definition indicates that the system of internal control does not provide reasonable assurance regarding the reliability of the financial statements.

COSO says:

"An effective system of internal control reduces, to an acceptable level, the risk of not achieving an objective relating to one, two, or all three categories. It requires that:

- Each of the five components of internal control and relevant principles is present and functioning

- The five components are operating together in an integrated manner

"In determining whether a system of internal control is effective, management exercises judgment in assessing whether each of the components and relevant principles is present and functioning and components are operating together."

For purposes of Sarbanes-Oxley, the "entity objective" is the filing of financial statements with the SEC that are free of material error. "An acceptable level" of the risk has been defined by the regulators as where the likelihood of a material misstatement of those financials is less than reasonably likely (see the discussion of materiality later).

Since management has to be based on a recognized framework, and COSO's *Internal Control – Integrated Framework* is the only specifically recognized framework, management has to be able to demonstrate (once the SEC has recognized the 2013 update as a replacement for the 1992 version) that:

1. The system of internal control provides reasonable assurance that the financial statements filed with the SEC will be free of material error, and

2. Each of the COSO components and relevant principles is present and functioning. (COSO has explained in the framework that the requirements concerning the components are satisfied if the relevant principles are present and functioning.)

The process for addressing these requirements is discussed in the following chapters.

WHO IS RESPONSIBLE FOR INTERNAL CONTROLS?

SECTIONS 302 AND 404 of Sarbanes-Oxley make it clear that management—specifically the CEO and CFO—is responsible for the adequacy of internal controls. The certification by these officers required by Section 302 states that:

"(4) the signing officers—

(A) are responsible for establishing and maintaining internal controls.

(B) have designed such internal controls to ensure that material information relating to the issuer and its consolidated subsidiaries is made known to such officers by others within those entities, particularly during the period in which the periodic reports are being prepared.

(C) have evaluated the effectiveness of the issuer's internal controls as of a date within 90 days prior to the report.

(D) have presented in the report their conclusions about the effectiveness of their internal controls based on their evaluation as of that date."

While the CEO and the executive team as a whole may look to the CFO for overall leadership and accountability for financial reporting, other parts of the organization have a significant part to play. For example, the system of ICFR typically includes processes in the procurement, inventory management, manufacturing, sales, and IT functions, many of which do not report to the CFO.

Responsibility for the system of internal control within a typical organization is a shared responsibility among all the executives, with leadership normally provided by the CFO.

The audit committee of the board of directors has a significant role in a company's system of internal control, which it performs on behalf of the full board and ultimately the shareholders. Specifically, the members:

- Provide oversight of management. COSO describes their role:

  "Management is responsible for the reliability of the financial statements, but an effective audit committee plays a critical oversight role. The board of directors, often through its audit committee, has the authority and responsibility to question senior management regarding how it is carrying out its internal and external reporting responsibilities and to verify that timely corrective actions are taken, as necessary."

  "As a result of its independence the audit committee, along with a strong internal audit function as applicable, is often best positioned to identify and promptly act in situations where senior management overrides controls or deviates from expected standards of conduct."

- Provide direction and oversight of the work of the external auditors, who are appointed by and report directly to the audit committee.

- Direct and oversee the performance of the internal audit activity, which typically reports to the audit committee.

In the United States, and increasingly in other countries, the external auditors are engaged by and directly accountable to the audit committee, a requirement of Sarbanes-Oxley. Through the external audit of the annual and review of the interim financial statements, and their audit of the system of internal control over financial reporting, the external auditors provide the audit committee, board of directors, investors, and management with assurance of the reliability of the financial statements. Although the external auditors provide assurance to the audit committee relative to the financial statements filed with the SEC, management is not permitted to place reliance on their work for purposes of Sarbanes-Oxley. Instead, management must have a system of internal control that is sufficient without relying on the external auditors.

By contrast, the internal audit activity is considered part of an organization's internal control system, even though it also is directly accountable to the audit committee in most public companies. While the chief audit executive (CAE) may report to a senior executive for administrative matters (preferably, the CEO), he or she should report functionally to the audit committee. The internal audit activity provides assurance to both management and the audit committee regarding the effectiveness of all aspects (i.e., not only financial but also operational effectiveness and compliance) of an organization's system of internal control, risk management, and governance practices.[1] Its activities are considered part of the "monitoring" component of the system of internal control and, therefore, are included in both management's and the external auditors' assessment. COSO describes their work:

> "As the third line of defense, internal auditors provide assurance and advisory support to management on internal control.... The internal audit activity includes evaluating the adequacy and effectiveness of controls in responding to risks within the organization's oversight, operations, and information systems regarding.... The scope of internal auditing is typically expected to include oversight, risk management, and internal control, and assist the organization in maintaining effective control by evaluating its effectiveness and efficiency and by promoting continual improvement. Internal audit communicates findings and interacts directly with management, the audit committee, and/or the board of directors."

The audit committee can and should rely on the assurances of management, internal auditors, and the external auditors in forming their own assessments and in approving financial statements that are filed with the SEC. Additional information on the role and responsibilities of each participant can be obtained from the company's CAE or The IIA.

The role of the internal auditor in the Sarbanes-Oxley program is discussed in chapter 15.

What is the Scope of Management's Assessment of the System of Internal Control Over Financial Reporting?

MANAGEMENT IS ACTUALLY required to provide multiple assessments of internal controls in its filings with the SEC. An assessment of *disclosure controls* is required by Section 302 and is included in quarterly and annual financial reports, while an assessment of internal control over financial reporting is required by Section 404 and is only included in annual reports.

When the SEC developed the detailed rules for implementing Section 302,[1] it required the CEO and CFO to make a number of statements relative to internal controls (i.e., the Section 302 certification). The SEC also required companies to include in their annual and quarterly financial statements an assessment of their *disclosure controls and procedures* (i.e., disclosure controls), a new term not actually mentioned in Sarbanes-Oxley. The SEC defined disclosure controls as:

> "...controls and other procedures that are designed to ensure that information required to be disclosed by the company in its Exchange Act reports is recorded, processed, summarized, and reported within the time periods specified in the Commission's rules and forms. Disclosure controls and procedures include, without limitation, controls and procedures designed to ensure that information required to be disclosed by the company in its Exchange Act reports is accumulated and communicated to the company's management (including its principal executive and financial officers) for timely assessment and disclosure pursuant to the SEC's rules and regulations."

A simple and practical definition of the scope of the Sarbanes-Oxley assessment is that it addresses the controls over everything in the GAAP-based (Generally Accepted

Accounting Principles) interim and annual financial statements and related notes that are filed with the SEC.[2]

Disclosure controls include these and more. They include controls over financial reporting, but extend beyond them to all information that is "required to be disclosed by the company in its Exchange Act reports." These reports include not only the financial statements and related footnotes but nonfinancial information as well. It is important to note that disclosure controls cover not just the quarterly and annual financial statements filed on Forms 10-Q and 10-K but also notifications of material events filed on Form 8-K or other current reports.[3] By contrast, Section 404 only relates to the financial information required to be included in filings with the SEC.

Disclosure controls include in their entirety all the Sarbanes-Oxley internal controls over financial reporting. Although the SEC in its early publications indicated that there would be significant overlap, in practice there are no key internal controls over financial reporting for Sarbanes-Oxley that are not part of disclosure controls.[4] On the other hand, there are significant areas covered under disclosure controls that are not part of ICFR. Examples of the latter include Management's Discussion and Analysis (MD&A) and the timely notification to investors using Form 8-K of material events.

Companies need not only (a) internal controls to ensure the completeness and accuracy of the financial information included in its filings with the SEC but also (b) internal controls to ensure the completeness, accuracy, and timeliness of nonfinancial information filed with the SEC. The combination of the two represents **disclosure controls**.

As a result:

- The assessment of disclosure controls can be that they are not effective, even though internal controls are effective (for example, due to issues surrounding the timely notification of material events to investors).

- If internal control over financial reporting is assessed as ineffective, disclosure controls cannot be considered effective.[5] This is because the financial information included in the filings with the SEC is the most critical part of those reports.

Section 302 requirements include, as mentioned above, a certification by the CEO and CFO and an assessment of its disclosure controls. The certification includes the following statements that relate to internal controls:

"4. The registrant's other certifying officer and I are responsible for establishing and maintaining disclosure controls and procedures (as defined in Exchange Act Rules 13a-15(e) and 15d-15(e)) and ICFR (as defined in Exchange Act Rules 13a-15(f) and 15d-15(f)) for the registrant and have:

(a) Designed such disclosure controls and procedures, or caused such disclosure controls and procedures to be designed under our supervision, to ensure that material information relating to the registrant, including its consolidated subsidiaries, is made known to us by others within those entities, particularly during the period in which this report is being prepared;

(b) Designed such internal control over financial reporting, or caused such ICFR to be designed under our supervision, to provide reasonable assurance regarding the reliability of financial reporting and the preparation of financial statements for external purposes in accordance with generally accepted accounting principles;

(c) Evaluated the effectiveness of the registrant's disclosure controls and procedures and presented in this report our conclusions about the effectiveness of the disclosure controls and procedures, as of the end of the period covered by this report based on such evaluation; and

(d) Disclosed in this report any change in the registrant's ICFR that occurred during the registrant's most recent fiscal quarter (the registrant's fourth fiscal quarter in the case of an annual report) that has materially affected, or is reasonably likely to materially affect, the registrant's internal control over financial reporting; and

"5. The registrant's other certifying officer and I have disclosed, based on our most recent evaluation of internal control over financial reporting, to the registrant's auditors and the audit committee of the registrant's board of directors (or persons performing the equivalent functions):

(a) All significant deficiencies and material weaknesses in the design or operation of ICFR which are reasonably likely to adversely affect the registrant's ability to record, process, summarize and report financial information; and

(b) Any fraud, whether or not material, that involves management or other employees who have a significant role in the registrant's internal control over financial reporting."

Clearly, there is a need to assess the adequacy of ICFR at interim periods to support the Section 302 certification and the annual assessment required by Section 404.

Major differences exist between the annual Sarbanes-Oxley assessment and that required for the interim Section 302 assessments:

- The external auditors do not provide an interim assessment[6] for Section 302.

- There is no current requirement that the rigor and formality required in practice for Sarbanes-Oxley be repeated each quarter for the Section 302 assessment. For example, it is not required that management test all or even a significant portion of its key controls each quarter. In addition, management's Section 302 process is not required to follow a recognized internal control framework.

However, prudence suggests that management:

- Has a reasonably formal, documented process for making the quarterly assessment that is included in the 10-Q and supports the Section 302 certifications.

  - I suggest that this can be included in the activities of the company's disclosure committee, which most of the larger companies have established.

  - The process should include the assessment of all internal control deficiencies known to management, including those identified not only during management's assessment process but also by either the external auditors in their Sarbanes-Oxley work or by internal audit in its various audit activities.

  - As discussed below, the system of ICFR must provide reasonable assurance with respect to the quarterly financial statements and the annual statements. The quarterly assessment is against a lower—typically one quarter the size—determination of what constitutes material.

- The process and results should be reviewed and discussed with the CEO and CFO to support their Section 302 certifications.

■ Confirms that the external auditors do not disagree with management's quarterly assessment.

■ Understands—which requires an appropriate process to gather the necessary information—whether there have been any major changes in the system of internal control during the quarter. A major change can include improvements and degradations in the system of internal control. While Section 302 only requires the disclosure in the 10-Q of a *material weakness* and the communication to the audit committee of a material or significant deficiency, the *correction* of a *significant* deficiency may be considered a major change and, if so, should be disclosed.

DEFINING THE DETAILED SCOPE FOR SARBANES-OXLEY

MANAGEMENT'S ASSESSMENT FOR Sarbanes-Oxley is as of year-end, so there may be a temptation to wait until late in the year before starting the program. However, there are important reasons for considering the program a continuing, year-round process and starting early each year:

- If there are issues relative either to the design or the consistent operation of the controls (i.e., exceptions will be identified during the testing), management will have time to make changes and retest successfully before year-end.

- Coordinating with the external auditors is generally easier if both are able to plan their work early in the year. Ideally, management and the auditors can agree on scope in time for this to be considered by the external auditors in fee proposals, scheduling staff with the global audit team, and so forth.

- Significant resources are required for testing that may be in short supply later in the year. Testing can be performed throughout the year spreading the resource burden. Note: If controls are tested early in the year, management must perform an update procedure to "roll forward" the results to year-end.

- The external auditors often have a policy requiring they start their testing only *after* management has tested and assessed the individual controls as effective. The earlier the external auditors perform their testing, the more time there is for management to remediate any issues and retest.

- In an integrated external audit, the external auditors often place a degree of reliance on the system of internal control over financial reporting for its financial statement audit (in addition to its Sarbanes-Oxley work). When management testing is spread across the year, rather than concentrated at year-end, the external auditors may be able to place some reliance on that testing and reduce its own work, resulting in a reduction in audit fees.

As explained above, spreading the testing provides management with improved assurance supporting the quarterly Section 302 certification and assessment of disclosure controls.

A. USING A TOP-DOWN AND RISK-BASED APPROACH TO DEFINING THE SCOPE

In defining the detailed scope for management's assessment (i.e., the controls that will be tested), a risk-based and top-down approach should be taken. As noted previously, the PCAOB requires such an approach in AS 5, and the SEC strongly recommends it in its guidance.

Both the PCAOB and the SEC provide principles-based guidance on the top-down approach, rather than a more prescriptive set of procedures.

AS 5 includes the following:

"The auditor should use a top-down approach to the audit of internal control over financial reporting to select the controls to test. A top-down approach begins at the financial statement level and with the auditor's understanding of the overall risks to internal control over financial reporting. The auditor then focuses on entity-level controls and works down to significant accounts and disclosures and their relevant assertions.[1]

"This approach directs the auditor's attention to accounts, disclosures, and assertions that present a reasonable possibility of material misstatement to the financial statements and related disclosures. The auditor then verifies his or her understanding of the risks in the company's processes and selects for testing those controls that sufficiently address the assessed risk of misstatement to each relevant assertion.

"Note: The top-down approach describes the auditor's sequential thought process in identifying risks and the controls to test, not necessarily the order in which the auditor will perform the auditing procedures."

The SEC uses different language, but the principles are the same:

"Management should evaluate whether it has implemented controls that will achieve the objective of ICFR (that is, to provide reasonable assurance regarding the reliability of financial reporting). The evaluation begins with the identification and assessment of the risks to reliable financial reporting (that is, materially accurate financial statements), including changes in those risks. Management then evaluates whether it has controls placed in operation (that is, in use) that are designed to adequately address those risks. Management ordinarily would consider the company's entity-level controls in both its assessment of risks and in identifying which controls adequately address the risks."

The SEC guidance continues with a high-level description of the steps involved:

- "Management should identify those risks of misstatement that could, individually or in combination with others, result in a material misstatement of the financial statements ("financial reporting risks"). Ordinarily, the identification of financial reporting risks begins with evaluating how the requirements of GAAP apply to the company's business, operations, and transactions."

- "Management uses its knowledge and understanding of the business, and its organization, operations, and processes, to consider the sources and potential likelihood of misstatements in financial reporting elements. Internal and external risk factors that impact the business, including the nature and extent of any changes in those risks, may give rise to a risk of misstatement. Risks of misstatement may also arise from sources such as the initiation, authorization, processing, and recording of transactions and other adjustments that are reflected in financial reporting elements. Management may find it useful to consider "what could go wrong" within a financial reporting element in order to identify the sources and the potential likelihood of misstatements and identify those that could result in a material misstatement of the financial statements."

- "Management's evaluation of the risk of misstatement should include consideration of the vulnerability of the entity to fraudulent activity (for example, fraudulent financial reporting, misappropriation of assets and corruption), and whether any such exposure could result in a material misstatement of the financial statements."

  "Management should recognize that the risk of material misstatement due to fraud ordinarily exists in any organization, regardless of size or type, and it may vary by specific location or segment and by individual financial reporting element. For example, one type of fraud risk that has resulted in fraudulent financial reporting in companies of all sizes and types is the risk of improper override of internal controls in the financial reporting process."

- "Management should evaluate whether it has controls placed in operation (that is, in use) that adequately address the company's financial reporting risks. The determination of whether an individual control, or a combination of controls, adequately addresses a financial reporting risk involves judgments about whether the controls, if operating properly, can effectively prevent or detect misstatements that could result in material misstatements in the financial statements."

  "Management may identify preventive controls, detective controls, or a combination of both, as adequately addressing financial reporting risks. There might be more than one control that addresses the financial reporting risks for a financial reporting element; conversely, one control might address the risks of more than one financial reporting element. It is not necessary to identify all controls that may exist or identify redundant controls, unless redundancy itself is required to address the financial reporting risks."

- "In addition to identifying controls that address the financial reporting risks of individual financial reporting elements, management also evaluates whether it has controls over the period-end financial reporting process, controls in place to address the entity-level and other pervasive elements of ICFR that its chosen control framework prescribes as necessary for an effective system of internal control. This would ordinarily include, for example, considering how and whether controls related to the control environment, controls over management override, the entity-level risk assessment process and monitoring activities, and the policies that address significant business control and risk management practices are adequate for purposes of an effective system of internal control."

Although this discussion was not carried forward to AS 5, AS 2 has an important section[2] on backup and contingency planning. Although many external audit firms ask for backup processes to be included in scope, I do not believe that to be the position of the regulators:

"Furthermore, management's plans that could potentially affect financial reporting in future periods are not controls. For example, a company's business continuity or contingency planning has no effect on the company's current abilities to initiate, authorize, record, process, or report financial data. Therefore, a company's business continuity or contingency planning is not part of internal control over financial reporting."

Another issue relating to scope pertains to whether acquisitions should be included in scope. SEC staff provided guidance on this question in its *Frequently Asked Questions* document (revised in 2007). Here are the question (Q) and answer (A):

"**Q:** If a registrant consummates a material purchase business combination during its fiscal year, must the internal control over financial reporting of the acquired business be included in management's report on internal control over financial reporting for that fiscal year?

"**A:**…we would typically expect management's report on internal control over financial reporting to include controls at all consolidated entities. However, we acknowledge that it might not always be possible to conduct an assessment of an acquired business's internal control over financial reporting in the period between the consummation date and the date of management's assessment. In such instances, we would not object to management referring in the report to a discussion in the registrant's Form 10-K or 10-KSB regarding the scope of the assessment and to such disclosure noting that management excluded the acquired business from management's report on internal control over financial reporting. If such a reference is made, however, management must identify the acquired business excluded and indicate the significance of the acquired business to the registrant's consolidated financial statements. Notwithstanding management's exclusion of an acquired business's internal controls from its annual assessment, a registrant must disclose any material change to its internal control over financial reporting due to the acquisition pursuant to Exchange Act Rule 13a-15(d) or 15d-15(d), whichever applies (also refer to the last two sentences in the answer to question 7). In addition, the period in which management may omit an assessment of an acquired business's internal control over financial reporting from its assessment of the registrant's internal control may not extend beyond one year from the date of acquisition, nor may such assessment be omitted from more than one annual management report on internal control over financial reporting."

B. Ensuring that the Assessment Process is Consistent with COSO's *Internal Control – Integrated Framework*

As noted above, the regulators require that the assessment of internal control over financial reporting for Sarbanes-Oxley compliance purposes be based upon a recognized internal control framework, and the only framework specifically recognized by the SEC is COSO's *Internal Control – Integrated Framework*. Therefore, it is important to follow a process that demonstrates consistency with the COSO framework.

The COSO framework specifies that for a system of internal control to be effective, it must (a) provide reasonable assurance that risks to the objective of filing financial statements with the SEC are free from reasonable error, and (b) all five components and relevant principles must be present and functioning.

Therefore, the process recommended below follows a top-down and risk-based approach and includes an assessment of all relevant principles from the COSO framework.

C. The Detailed Process for Defining the Scope

The suggested process, shown below, is consistent with the principles discussed above and with guidance from the SEC and PCAOB. At a high level, it involves:

a. Identifying and assessing the sources of risk to the financial statements. With respect to the COSO framework, this is addressed in the Risk Assessment component and its principles (i.e., principles 6-9 above). Steps include identifying:

- The general ledger accounts that constitute each line in the financial statements as filed. For example, accounts payable is normally one line in the financial statements, although it represents a group of related general ledger accounts.

- For each of the above, the accounts that are considered significant.

- The financial statement assertions relevant to those accounts and material to the investor.

- The locations to include in scope.

- The business processes that process transactions into the significant accounts at in-scope locations.

- The key transactions representing balances in the above accounts.

b. Identifying those controls that have a direct effect on the likelihood of material misstatement, either by preventing or detecting material errors or omissions. These are referred to in this book as "direct controls" (a term not used in regulatory guidance, although the latter does talk about controls that only have an "indirect effect"). The majority of the direct controls are typically in the Control Activities component (principles 10-12 apply).

c. Obtaining a self-assessment from management of each of the COSO principles. I am going to assume, being prudent, that all 17 are considered "relevant" for our purposes.

d. Performing a risk assessment for each of the COSO principles.

e. Where a defect in the presence or functioning of any of these principles is at least reasonably likely to lead to the failure of one or more direct key controls, rate it as high risk and identify the key controls that will be relied upon for each principle. Otherwise, rate it as a low risk and rely on management's self-assessment of the principles. (See detailed discussion below.)

f. Performing a "reasonable person" review. Would a reasonable person believe that the set of key controls that has been included in scope would, if adequately designed and operating effectively, provide the reasonable assurance desired?

D. Potential Changes in the Business

Because so much will depend on whether the system of internal control provides reasonable assurance that a material error will be either prevented or detected, the place to start the detailed process is a definition of *material error,* or the level of *materiality.* However, a prerequisite to that first step is to consider the potential for changes to the business during the upcoming year.

Companies and the business environment within which they operate do not stand still. Rather than relying exclusively on the prior year's financials to set the new year's Sarbanes-Oxley scope, management should consider the potential for change, such as:

- Changes in revenue levels, margins, gross profits, and other financial results that might impact how materiality is determined.

- Changes in how the company conducts its operations, including where sales are generated, how products are manufactured, what computer systems are used, whether processes are outsourced or managed at shared service centers, and so forth. These might indicate that important business processes for Sarbanes-Oxley and the related key controls might change.

- Changes in key personnel that might indicate the risk of control failure is increased (such as when experienced personnel are replaced).

- Changes in the regulatory environment that might indicate changes will be made to important business processes.

During planning, the scope for the Sarbanes-Oxley program is normally based on the anticipated results for the year and which will be sources of risk (such as which will be the significant accounts and locations). Management should continue to monitor this throughout the year to ensure that the scope of the Sarbanes-Oxley program remains appropriate.

E. Materiality

There is guidance in the accounting and auditing literature on this topic that is lengthy (and not repeated here), but it comes down to a fairly simple test: what would be material to the reasonable investor when making an investment decision in the company's securities? Usually, this is 5 percent of the company's pre-tax net income, but it may be different when the company has losses or low profit levels; both quantitative and qualitative aspects must be considered.

In August 2010, the PCAOB released a series of auditing standards related to the auditor's assessment or, and response to, risk in an audit. Auditing Standard 11, *Consideration of Materiality in Planning and Performing an Audit*, includes these two paragraphs:

- "In interpreting the federal securities laws, the Supreme Court of the United States has held that a fact is material if there is 'a substantial likelihood that the ...fact would have been viewed by the reasonable investor as having significantly altered the 'total mix' of information made available.' As the Supreme Court has noted, determinations of materiality require 'delicate assessments of the inferences a 'reasonable shareholder' would draw from a given set of facts and the significance of those inferences to him....'"

- "To plan the nature, timing, and extent of audit procedures, the auditor should establish a materiality level for the financial statements as a whole that is appropriate in light of the particular circumstances. This includes consideration of the company's earnings and other relevant factors. To determine the nature, timing, and extent of audit procedures, the materiality level for the financial statements as a whole needs to be expressed as a specified amount."

It is preferable if the external auditors agree with management's determination of materiality, so early discussions should be held. The external auditors may indicate that only a preliminary determination may be made, as facts may change before the end of the year.

The determination of materiality for Sarbanes-Oxley should consider:

- The level of error that would be material to the full year's results if it affects the income statement.[3]

- Not all errors affect the profit and loss (P&L); some only impact the balance sheet. In a few cases, the errors are in the disclosures (e.g., footnotes or earnings per share calculations). These errors will have to be assessed on their specific facts and circumstances.

- In all cases, a bright-line definition must be tempered with an assessment of what a reasonable investor might conclude. It is easy to rush to judgment and label an error material that would have no effect on any investor's assessment of the company.

This determination of what would be material for the annual financials should be made by technical accounting personnel after discussion with the external auditors. The determination should consider both quantitative and qualitative factors.

> **KEY POINTS:**
> WORKING WITH
> EXTERNAL AUDITORS
>
> ► Management should work closely with the external auditor at every stage of their Section 404 process.
>
> ► Management's materiality will influence the external auditor's own level, which can have implications on the extent of testing and related costs.

Management should work closely with the external auditors at every stage of the Sarbanes-Oxley process (see chapter 14) and materiality is an important agreement to make. Management's level should influence the external auditor's own level, which can have implications on the extent of testing and cost (both for management testing and external auditor fees).

F. Significant Accounts and Disclosures

Having decided on a materiality level for the full year's P&L, management needs to determine how and where an error could occur. The financial statements are examined to determine in which accounts and disclosures there is the possibility of a material error. These are considered "significant accounts."[4]

It should be noted that the SEC guidance does not include, as a step, the identification of significant accounts or locations, business processes, or major classes of transactions. Instead, it suggests that management identify financial reporting risks and the controls required to address those risks. The steps discussed here provide a process for identifying the risk of material misstatement of the financials (i.e., financial reporting risks) and related key controls.

Any account that has a larger balance than the materiality level should be given strong consideration as a significant account, as there is at least a possibility that it could contain a misstatement that would be material to the financial statements. Management should also take into account the possibility that account balances will be higher at year-end (e.g., reflecting planned revenue growth).

Accounts that are small and highly unlikely to contain an error of a material amount can usually be excluded from the scope for Sarbanes-Oxley. AS 5 advises that "the maximum amount that an account balance or total of transactions can be overstated is generally the recorded amount, while understatements could be larger." Absent qualitative factors (e.g., whether the account balance fluctuates significantly from period to period, or involves complex accounting with a significant level of judgment), accounts with balances less than the materiality level can generally be excluded from scope as being unlikely to contain a material error.[5]

An important exception is where multiple small accounts are subject to a *single point of failure* and as a group exceed the materiality level. For example, a company may have multiple accounts for different types of finished goods inventory (e.g., a retailer with different accounts for domestic appliances, hardware, and clothing). However, it may use the same processes for all finished goods inventory accounting and a failure in a single control could affect multiple accounts. In this case, management should group these related accounts and consider them all as significant.

Auditing Standard 11 discusses the concept of *tolerable misstatement*. Because a single failure of internal control can result in errors in multiple accounts that in aggregate exceed materiality, they direct the auditor to establish a materiality level for individual accounts that is lower than the level of a material misstatement. This tolerable misstatement level is then used in determining which accounts are significant and should be in scope.

This is the relevant section of AS 11:

> "The auditor should determine the amount or amounts of tolerable misstatement for purposes of assessing risks of material misstatement and planning and performing audit procedures at the account or disclosure level. The auditor should determine tolerable misstatement at an amount or amounts that reduce to an appropriately low level the probability that the total of uncorrected and undetected misstatements would result in material misstatement of the financial statements. Accordingly, tolerable misstatement should be less than the materiality level for the financial statements as a whole and, if applicable, the materiality level or levels for particular accounts or disclosures."

Management may follow the same approach or use its knowledge of the organization's processes and controls to include this consideration as a qualitative risk factor in the selection of significant accounts. However, management should work with the auditor to ensure that the latter does not set an unreasonably low level of tolerable misstatement—as that will result in unnecessary testing and expense. For example, if the auditor establishes tolerable misstatement levels at 80 percent of materiality across all accounts, management should ask the auditor to explain why. AS 11 instructs the auditor to have a reasonable basis for tolerable misstatement:

> "In determining tolerable misstatement and planning and performing audit procedures, the auditor should take into account the nature, cause (if known), and amount of misstatements that were accumulated in audits of the financial statements of prior periods."

The grouping of accounts can also work to reduce the number of significant accounts. For example, fixed assets and accumulated depreciation may individually exceed the materiality level. However, they are reported together in the financial statements and management may determine that the risk of a material misstatement of *net* fixed assets is unlikely. A similar situation may occur with other accounts that tend to offset when combined for financial reporting purposes (e.g., intangibles and related amortization).

The scope of Sarbanes-Oxley extends to the notes and other disclosures that are part of the financial statements. Management needs to perform a risk assessment on all of the notes to determine which are significant and the nature and magnitude of an error that would be considered material to the investor. That determination may affect the selection of which accounts to include in scope, perhaps including some accounts that are below the agreed materiality.

Materiality and the accounts in scope should be assessed at least quarterly, or when there are material changes in the business, to ensure there is no need to add or remove areas from scope.

G. FINANCIAL STATEMENT ASSERTIONS

The external auditing profession has identified a number of financial statement assertions that may be applicable to the selected general ledger accounts. AS 5 requires the external auditor to determine which of these are *relevant* (i.e., a potential source of misstatement). Management may decide to follow the same process and ensure all relevant assertions for each significant account are addressed by appropriate key controls. (At some companies, management has not found using assertions in the scoping exercise to be valuable. However, it can be useful to demonstrate consistency with the external auditor's process.)

The assertions suggested by AS 5 are as follows:

- **Existence or Occurrence** addresses whether assets or liabilities exist at a given date and whether recorded transactions have occurred during a given period.

- **Completeness** addresses whether all transactions and accounts that should be presented in the financial statements are so included.

- **Valuation or Allocation** addresses whether asset, liability, equity, revenue, and expense components are included in the financial statements at appropriate amounts.

- **Rights and Obligations** relates to whether the rights and liabilities are the obligations of the entity at a given date.

- **Presentation and Disclosure** addresses whether particular components of the financial statements are properly classified, described, and disclosed.

H. SIGNIFICANT LOCATIONS, BUSINESS PROCESSES, AND MAJOR CLASSES OF TRANSACTIONS

The majority of companies have operations in multiple locations, and an analysis should be performed to identify those locations that are *significant*. It should be performed separately for each significant account, as follows:

- For each significant account, identify those locations whose transactions are involved.

- Determine whether there is at least a reasonable possibility of a material error resulting from that location's transactions in the significant account. If so, that location is significant for that account.

- For locations that are not significant for an account, assess whether there are multiple locations that should be aggregated for risk assessment purposes. For example, if transactions for several locations share a common process and rely on the same control, the failure of that common control could result in misstatements in multiple locations that are individually not material but that are material in the aggregate.

Note that this process generally results in the selection of different significant accounts in each location. The key is to select the combination of location and account where there is at least a reasonable possibility of a material error. For example, a company may have 20 significant accounts; five of those accounts may be a potential source of a material error (because only these five are large enough) at location A, while location B has 10 accounts in scope, and location C has all 20.

AS 5 includes a short but useful paragraph of guidance:[6]

"In determining the locations or business units at which to perform tests of controls, the auditor should assess the risk of material misstatement to the financial statements associated with the location or business unit and correlate the amount of audit attention devoted to the location or business unit with the degree of risk.

"Note: The auditor may eliminate from further consideration locations or business units that, individually or when aggregated with others, do not present a reasonable possibility of material misstatement to the company's consolidated financial statements."

AS 11 takes this further:

"For purposes of the audit of the consolidated financial statements of a company with multiple locations or business units, the auditor should determine tolerable misstatement for the individual locations or business units at an amount that reduces to an appropriately low level the probability that the total of uncorrected and undetected misstatements would result in material misstatement of the consolidated financial statements. Accordingly, tolerable misstatement at an individual location should be less than the materiality level for the financial statements as a whole."

> **KEY POINT:**
> **MULTIPLE LOCATIONS**
>
> "The auditor may eliminate from further consideration locations or business units that, individually or when aggregated with others, do not present a reasonable possibility of material misstatement to the company's consolidated financial statements."
>
> (Auditing Standard Number 5)

However, any tolerable misstatement at an individual location must be a reasonable level, based on the likelihood that errors would be made at multiple locations, in the same direction and the same or related accounts, due to a common control failure.

One point that comes up occasionally is the intersection of (a) the audit of the corporate financial statements and the assessment of the system of internal control over financial reporting, and (b) the statutory audit of a subsidiary. The local external audit team may discuss and suggest a scope that is based on local rather than corporate materiality. The local materiality, of course, will be lower and bring more accounts into scope. However useful that may be for the local auditors and their statutory audit, the expanded scope is not necessary for the corporate Sarbanes-Oxley work. Testing additional controls should be discussed at the local level to ensure the value of any management testing is clear and the work justified.

The balances in the significant accounts are the result of transactions that flow through a number of business processes. For each significant account and location combination, the key business processes now need to be identified.[8]

I recommend identifying which transactions constitute the preponderance of the account balances and which represent a reasonably possible source of material misstatement. That will enable a focus on those material transactions together with the related processes and controls, and the exclusion of immaterial transactions that flow into significant accounts. For example, the significant account for depreciation may include not only the depreciation of plant and equipment, but also the depreciation of company vehicles. For most companies, depreciation of the small number of company vehicles is not material either to the P&L or the balance sheet and should be excluded from Sarbanes-Oxley scope.

Another example is when there are returns for defective product that result in credit memos. While these may flow into significant accounts, for some companies the level of returns and their value is small and there is no real risk that a material error could be the result of credit memos. Processes and controls over insignificant, trivial transactions can be excluded from scope. The scope should be limited to those accounts, locations, and transactions where there is a reasonable possibility of material misstatement.

At this point, management has defined materiality and identified:

- The significant general ledger accounts and notes to be included in scope.

- At which locations the controls and processes related to those accounts will be assessed and tested.

- The business processes and material transactions that constitute the balances in those accounts.

I. KEY CONTROLS

The next step is to identify which controls will be included in scope and tested. While management can opt to test many controls, the most efficient Sarbanes-Oxley program will be one that focuses on the limited set of controls required to provide reasonable assurance that material misstatements of the financials will either be prevented or detected timely.

- AS 5 states: "The auditor…selects for testing those controls that sufficiently address the assessed risk of misstatement."

- SEC staff guidance is similar: "The overall focus of internal control reporting should be on those items that could result in material errors in the financial statements."

The SEC guidance made this telling statement: "Management should not allow the goal and purpose of the internal control provisions—the production of reliable financial statements—to be overshadowed by the process."

The controls that are necessary and relied upon are called *key controls*.

Although referenced in some PCAOB documents, including its November 30, 2005, report[9] on the initial implementation of AS 2, there is no commonly accepted definition of a key control. I support the following, which I believe is consistent with PCAOB and SEC published guidance:

A key control is a control that, if it fails, means there is at least a reasonable likelihood that a material error in the financial statements would not be prevented or detected on a timely basis. In other words, a key control is one that is required to provide reasonable assurance that material errors will be prevented or timely detected.

Careful identification of key controls is important to an efficient and effective Sarbanes-Oxley program. An overly conservative approach, where too many controls are defined as *key*, will result in excessive time and resources testing controls that are not critical to the assessment.

It is important to note that there is no generic "laundry list" of what will always be considered a key control and, due to differences in systems, procedures, business environments, and models, sound professional judgment is required during the identification process. Management should also give due consideration to the views of the external auditors and ensure they are comfortable with the process management uses for identifying key controls.

There is also no magic number—no ideal quantity of key controls. While some have looked to surveys to see how many key controls other companies have identified, there is no such thing as a "best practice" number. Each company must identify its own financial reporting risks and the controls it relies on to manage them. The number of controls will be affected by such matters as:

- The number of significant accounts and locations.

- The materiality level, especially relative to the size of typical transactions.

- The level of standardized processes and systems, including the existence of shared service centers.

- The diversity of the business.

- The quality of entity-level controls and their ability to address financial reporting risks and reduce the number of activity-level controls.

Ernst & Young completed a survey in 2011[10] that included some statistics on the number of total Sarbanes-Oxley-related controls and, of those, the number of key controls. This table summarizes the results:

RESPONDENTS %	SARBANES-OXLEY-RELATED CONTROLS	KEY CONTROLS (%)	KEY CONTROLS
19%	Less than 250	79%	Less than 200
24%	250–499	78%	200–400
22%	500–999	72%	400–720
22%	1,000–2,499	66%	720–1,650
13%	2,500 or more	62%	1,550 or more

The authors also commented that 35 percent of the participants in the study have more than 1,000 Sarbanes-Oxley-related controls, of which more than 60 percent are considered key controls.

It is very difficult to draw any conclusions from these statistics. My last two companies reported:

- A $4 billion global manufacturer of hard drives had 1,100 key controls.

- A $1.5 billion global software company had 500 key controls.

The only observation that I would make from the Ernst & Young study is that companies had identified a large percentage of the total Sarbanes-Oxley-related controls as key controls. This is likely to indicate that further efficiencies could be obtained by streamlining using the top-down approach recommended here.

Controls may either prevent errors or detect their occurrence. Some experts include the determination of whether controls are preventive or detective in their process to identify key controls, because preventive controls are seen as stronger. However, management should recognize that an efficient and effective system of controls will use a *combination* of both, and I do not consider it critical to focus on whether controls are one or the other. Rather, management should focus on whether the controls in place are sufficient to ensure there are no misstatements of the financials and are appropriate in terms of managing business risk.

Often, key controls will be within business processes at a third party (e.g., an outsourced shared service center, or a payroll processing company). At this point, these controls should be included in the scoping as if they were in-house. Where there is a choice to select in-house or third-party operated key controls to address a financial reporting risk, management should consider such factors as its ability to obtain an SSAE 16/SOC 1 report (previously, a SAS 70 Type II report) as discussed in chapter 7 (f) and the quality of the controls and the risk they may not function consistently (e.g., where there is a significant level of staff turnover, or inexperienced management).

The identification of key controls should take into account the risk of fraud, including the override by management of controls. It is important to remember that while the prevention of fraud (or at least its detection) is important to the business, only the risk of fraud that results in a material misstatement of the financials must be included in the Sarbanes-Oxley assessment (see the Fraud Risk Assessment section in chapter 7).

The SEC's and PCAOB's guidance describes the top-down approach in a way that implies that entity-level controls should be understood and considered first, before understanding business process controls (at the activity level). In its 2006 review of external auditors' work, the PCAOB said, "The inspectors also observed more instances in which auditors approached the audit of internal control from the top down and thus did a better job of focusing their testing and evaluation on the relevant company-level controls. As a result, they spent less time testing a larger number of controls that existed at the process, transaction, and application levels."

> **KEY POINT:**
> FRAUD
>
> Only the risk of fraud that results in a material misstatement of the financials must to be included in the Sarbanes-Oxley assessment.

However, AS 5 points out that "The top-down approach describes the auditor's sequential thought process in identifying risks and the controls to test, not necessarily the order in which the auditor will perform the auditing procedures."

In addition, there are two types of entity-level controls: those that have a *direct* impact on the integrity of financial reporting (such as the review of variances from forecast by a corporate financial analyst), and those whose impact is *indirect* (such as the oversight of financial reporting by the audit committee of the board). *Direct* entity-level controls may be key controls that are relied on to prevent or detect material misstatements. *Indirect* entity-level controls are also important but only because poor indirect entity-level controls indicate a higher risk that key controls will not operate as required.

I believe that the key controls that should be considered first are the *direct* key controls, whether within business processes or at the entity-level. They have a direct effect on the risk of material misstatement. Once the *direct* key controls have been identified, *indirect* key controls should be considered. As explained earlier, indirect key controls are best identified (a) for COSO principles that are high risk, and (b) after the population of direct key controls has been identified.

1. Identifying Direct Key Controls Within Business Processes

It is important to recognize that sometimes several controls are required to work as a *combination* to provide assurance on one financial reporting risk on the transactions that flow into one account. The controls may operate at the same level (e.g., at the activity level, such as the preparation of a bank reconciliation by a staff member and its separate review and approval by a manager) or function at different levels (e.g., at the entity and activity levels, such as the posting of a journal entry by the controller at a division and a review by the corporate controller during the period-end close to ensure all major journal entries were posted).

The following process is recommended. It should deliver a scope that is sufficient to address the risk of material misstatement and includes an efficient number of key controls.

1. The selection should start by assessing whether there are any key controls at the *entity level* that would be sufficient to prevent or detect a material misstatement relating to a significant account at a significant location. When such *direct* controls exist and are effective, management may determine there is no need to identify controls at lower levels. AS 5 explains:

   "Some entity-level controls might be designed to operate at a level of precision that would adequately prevent or detect on a timely basis misstatements to one or more relevant assertions. If an entity-level control sufficiently addresses the assessed risk of misstatement, the auditor need not test additional controls relating to that risk."

An example of this situation might be the controls over payroll expense at a manufacturing company. If headcount is relatively stable and fluctuations are well below materiality levels, a high-level review performed as part of the period-end close process might be sufficient to detect any significant error. In that case, activity-level controls, such as those within the payroll business process over adding employees to payroll and changing salary and deduction information, probably will not need to be tested as key controls.

It should be noted that high-level reviews such as this are not necessarily performed at the company or entity level. They may be performed at the location itself, a regional headquarters, a shared service center, or at the corporate level.

2. The next step is to determine whether there are detective controls, similar to entity-level controls but operating at an *intermediate level* (e.g., regional, shared service center, or local management level), that

provide reasonable assurance that material errors would be detected timely.

As with entity-level controls, effective intermediate-level controls may be sufficient by themselves, and controls within the activity not included as key controls.

3. If insufficient controls are identified at higher levels, *activity-level controls* should be reviewed and key controls identified.

Key controls, regardless of the level at which they operate (entity, intermediate, or activity), vary in how they work.

- Some controls are fully manual, such as the inspection of incoming materials for quality.

- Some key business controls are fully automated (for example, the calculation of interest for banks or updating the correct general ledger account).

- Some controls are partly automated—also known as *hybrid* controls. For most companies, a large number of controls are of this type, where the individual performing the control relies on a report from the organization's primary business application, a data warehouse, or information on a computer screen. An example of this is the bank reconciliation, where the control uses reports from the general ledger system listing the cash balance and the various transactions that took place during the month. The reconciliation to the bank statement provides assurance that the reports are correct.

  Hybrid controls must be examined carefully. If the normal operation of the manual portion of the control is sufficient to detect an error in the automated part (e.g., the computer report), then the control should be treated as entirely manual because no reliance is being placed on the computer system. For example, the bank reconciliation might use a report from the general ledger system of cash transactions; if the report was incorrect or incomplete, it would be detected by the bank reconciliation process.

  However, if the automated part of the control is not assured by the manual part, then it will have to be tested as an automated control.

An example of a report that requires further testing is a report of all transactions over a defined dollar limit. The individual reviewing and taking action on this report cannot know that the report is complete and lists all items over the threshold. Therefore, the report should be tested as an automated control.

Key controls using a form of user computing, such as spreadsheets, may require special attention.[11]

Some organizations have separated the identification of manual and automated controls, with the finance function (or financial internal auditors) identifying the manual controls and the IT function (or IT auditors) identifying the automated controls. This approach is likely to lead to *significant problems* because it is not top down. It can result in the identification of redundant controls (two controls, one manual and one automated, where only one is needed) or the failure to include the best combination of controls to address financial reporting risks. Experience has shown that when IT auditors or management identify IT-related controls, they very often identify more controls than are necessary.

Instead, the identification of IT controls—both automated controls within business processes and IT general controls—should be the result of a top-down approach. The team performing the identification should have a solid understanding of the financial statements, business processes, and IT. This is the only realistic path to defining a scope that is not only sufficient to address financial reporting risks, but is efficient.

2. Segregation of Duties

Segregation of duties (SOD) and restricted access (RA) controls must be identified, assessed, and tested where they are key controls. Key SOD and RA controls include those that:

- Are required for an authorization control to be effective. For example, if the business control requires that all purchase orders be approved in the system by the purchasing manager, it is critical to ensure that only the purchasing manager has that capability.

- Reduce the risk of a material fraud that could be reported incorrectly in the financial statements.

With restricted access and segregation of duties, there is a risk of doing more work than is required for Sarbanes-Oxley. While there are excellent business reasons for restricting access to only those functions individuals need to perform their assigned tasks, it is important to remember that only fraud risk that is both material and also misstated in the financials is within scope for Sarbanes-Oxley. See the Fraud Risk section below.

This last point is important. Many companies test SOD using a standard set of "rules" (combinations of access privileges deemed inappropriate) provided by a consultant or vendor. While they may represent a *risk* to the business (at least in theory), they may not represent a risk of material misstatement for your organization. The rules used to drive SOD testing should be based on the top-down, risk-based approach described above to support a key control or reduce the risk of a material fraud.

As an example, at a company where I was responsible for the Sarbanes-Oxley program, both the external auditor and the internal auditor (at that point, the internal audit activity was outsourced) had tested user access consistently for several years. They each used a standard set of more than 150 rules to identify (a) access to important ERP transactions, and (b) SOD conflicts where one individual would have the ability, using a combination of ERP transactions, to commit a fraud. When the Sarbanes-Oxley team changed to a risk-based approach, concentrating on testing access rights that represented a risk of material misstatement, the number of rules was cut to about 20.

3. *Identifying Key IT General Controls*

When there is reliance on key automated controls (or on hybrid controls where failures in the automated part of the control might not be detected by the manual part), an assessment should be made to determine risks within IT general controls processes and identify key IT general controls (ITGC).

Broadly speaking, ITGC provide assurance that applications are developed and subsequently maintained, such that they provide the functionality required to process transactions and provide automated controls. They also assure the proper operation of the applications and the protection of both data and programs from unauthorized change.

The challenge to identifying the optimal combination of key controls within ITGC is that they do not have a direct effect on the financial statements. Because they provide assurance of the continued, proper operation of key automated controls, a failure in a key ITGC control implies the loss of that assurance. In other words, reliance on ITGC is indirect—through reliance on key automated controls. If ITGC key controls fail, key automated controls may not be reliable; if they are not reliable, they might fail to perform their function of preventing or detecting a material error.

A key ITGC control meets the definition of a key control provided earlier: "A key control is a control that, if it fails, means there is at least a reasonable likelihood that a material error in the financial statements would not be prevented or detected on a timely basis. In other words, a key control is one that is required to provide reasonable assurance that material errors will be prevented or timely detected." The difference is that the risk is indirect, through a lack of assurance over a key automated control.

A control within ITGC is, therefore, only key if it is linked to an identified key automated (or hybrid) control *and* relied on to provide assurance of the continued, proper operation of that key control. Otherwise, failures in the ITGC control would not result in the failure of a key automated control and, therefore, not represent a risk of material error in the financial statements.

The SEC guidance reinforces this:

> "For purposes of the evaluation of ICFR, management only needs to evaluate those IT general controls that are necessary for the proper and consistent operation of other controls designed to adequately address financial reporting risks."

Key controls in ITGC are, as a result, best identified through a continuation of the top-down, risk-based approach described here and in SEC and PCAOB guidance. The top-down approach identifies all the key automated controls that will be relied on. The top-down approach continues by identifying risks within ITGC processes (such as change management, security, or operations) to those key automated controls and the key controls within the ITGC processes necessary to address those risks. To quote the SEC again:

> "The identification of risks and controls within IT should not be a separate evaluation. Instead, it should be an integral part of management's

top-down, risk-based approach to identifying risks and controls and in determining evidential matter necessary to support the assessment."

Some organizations have developed the ITGC portion of their Sarbanes-Oxley scope based on a list of desired ITGC controls, or on what have been defined as critical based on general principles. While all of these controls may be important to the business and internal control as a whole, they may not all be critical or key controls for Sarbanes-Oxley purposes.

It is essential that the ITGC portion of the Sarbanes-Oxley scope be defined using a top-down approach that focuses on the risk of material misstatement. Otherwise, experience has shown that not only are too many ITGC controls identified as key (which increases the cost of the Sarbanes-Oxley program), but there may be a failure to identify the right controls. For example, at a company where I was responsible for internal audit and Sarbanes-Oxley program management, I initiated a top-down, risk-based scoping exercise for ITGC key controls. One key automated control concerned the pricing of sales orders. The exercise found that the software involved in the pricing was not actually maintained by the IT department but by a unit in the engineering function. The ITGC key controls related to that piece of software were not within IT but in engineering. In addition to adding a number of ITGC controls within engineering, the exercise also resulted in removing several ITGC controls (such as controls over maintenance of network router configurations) from scope because they were not relied on for any key automated controls.

The IIA has published a Guide to the Assessment of IT Risk (GAIT)[12] Methodology that provides detailed guidance on how risks should be identified as a continuation of the top-down approach, as presented in this document. GAIT is consistent with the PCAOB's and SEC's guidance and has been adopted by a growing number of organizations and their external auditors. The following discussion is based on the methodology, which should be referenced for more detailed guidance. (ISACA and the IT Governance Institute can generally be relied on for excellent guidance around IT issues. Unfortunately, they have not updated their 2006 guidance related to

> **KEY POINT:**
> SEC GUIDANCE ON ITGC
>
> "For purposes of the evaluation of ICFR, management only needs to evaluate those IT general controls that are necessary for the proper and consistent operation of other controls designed to adequately address financial reporting risks."

Sarbanes-Oxley—*IT Control Objectives for Sarbanes-Oxley: The Role of IT in the Design and Implementation of Internal Control Over Financial Reporting, 2nd Edition*—to reflect the top-down, risk-based approach and AS 5. ISACA's COBIT framework is recommended in GAIT and here as useful in selecting control objectives in step 3 below.)

Failure to define the scope of ITGC carefully can result in both too much work (by testing controls that are not really key) and failing to address all the risks to key automated controls. In addition, IT general control processes can be extensive and include a significant number of controls relative to the development, maintenance, and operation of applications and infrastructure (e.g., operating systems and databases) and the security of the computer network, applications, and data. Due to the technical nature of IT general controls and the changing threats to network security, it is difficult for IT management to design and operate controls that are fully effective.[13] As a result, IT management in many organizations has incurred significant costs, including personnel and software, to ensure IT general controls are adequately designed and operated. If the scope of IT general control that is relied upon for Sarbanes-Oxley is too broad, the assessment cost can be significant.

I recommend that management use the following process for identifying key controls within IT general control processes:

1. **Identify, and validate, if necessary, critical IT functionality.**

Critical IT functionality[14] refers to functions performed by application software that must function consistently and appropriately if material errors are to be prevented or detected. They include:

- Automated controls.

- The automated portion of hybrid controls.

- Other functionality that is not technically a control, but is necessary. Examples include complex calculations in a manufacturing company's warranty reserve, the aging of an accounts receivable report, the protection of information used in preparing the financial statements (i.e., data security), or the updating of transactions to the general ledger.

In this step, a careful review is performed to ensure all the critical functionality has been identified. Experience shows that while automated controls are easy to identify, the other two may not be. In addition, this is an opportunity to confirm that there is no unnecessary duplication of coverage between multiple controls, including situations where both manual and automated controls provide sufficient assurance. In these cases, management can select which key controls will be tested and included in scope.

Critical IT functionality is not limited to enterprise applications. It may be found in:

- Spreadsheets and other end-user applications.

- Data analytics or business intelligence applications.

- Applications that are not maintained by IT, but by another function (for example, an application maintained by the customer service function that is used to calculate warranty reserves).

2. Identify the significant applications where IT general controls should be tested.

Significant applications are those where either:

a. There is critical IT functionality, or

b. Transactions are processed and stored and an unauthorized change (including addition or deletion) of the data might not be detected by business processes controls *and* could result in a material misstatement of the financials.

While there may be risk to business operations if IT general controls relating to other applications fail, such failure would not result in a material error in the financial statements.

Step 1 resulted in a list of all the critical IT functionality. The list is now sorted by application to identify the significant applications. These are the applications that may be a source of risk. The risk is a failure in developing, maintaining, securing, or using the application could cause critical functionality to fail. To repeat: if an application does not contain any critical IT functionality, related IT general controls do not need to be assessed and tested.

3. Identify IT general control process risks and related control objectives.

For each significant application, the IT general control processes (e.g., change management, security, and operations) should be examined for risks. If a failure in one of those processes would be at least reasonably likely to result in a failure of a critical IT functionality, then the related IT control objectives should be identified (e.g., all application code changes are approved).

As explained in detail in GAIT, an ITGC process failure only represents a risk that needs to be addressed if it would result in either the failure of critical IT functionality or the undetected change of data that leads to a material misstatement. For example, a defect in change control processes for an application would not be in scope if that application did not contain critical functionality and the only risk is an unauthorized change to data maintained by the system.

> **KEY POINT:**
> SIGNIFICANT APPLICATIONS
>
> If an application does not contain any critical IT functionality, related IT general controls do not need to be assessed and tested.

It is important to recognize that just because an application is considered *significant* and "in scope," it is not necessary to test *every* related ITGC process. The only ones that must be included in scope are where a failure in the process represents a risk to critical functionality or material change to data.

Each organization will identify risks and related control objectives specific to its own facts and circumstances, because it depends on what it identifies as critical IT functionality.

Examples of ITGC process risks and related IT control objectives are shown below:

- In a manufacturing company, a key automated control is the three-way match between purchase orders, records of goods received, and the vendors' invoices. The significant application containing this critical IT functionality is the company's financial system. Using the GAIT Methodology, management determines that a failure to properly approve, test, and make changes to the code might result in a failure of the three-way match to operate appropriately. Then, the IT control objectives are identified: (a) "all changes to the financial system are properly approved"; (b) "all changes to the financial system are adequately tested";

> **KEY POINT:**
> SIGNIFICANT APPLICATIONS
> AND ITGC
>
> Just because an application is considered *significant* and "in scope," it is not necessary to test every related ITGC process.

and (c) "changes to the financial system are accurately placed into production."

- An insurance company relies on historical records of claims received in the calculation of reserves. It determines that inappropriate changes to that data might result in errors in the reserve calculation that would not be detected. Protection of the data is seen as critical IT functionality; the risk is that the data might be changed, and the IT control objective is that "only approved changes are made to the historical record of claims."

Many companies have included more ITGC-related testing in their Sarbanes-Oxley program scope than is necessary. To repeat:

- ITGC risks should be defined based on a top-down, risk-based approach that starts with risks of material misstatement to the financials.

- The only ITGC process risks that must be addressed for Sarbanes-Oxley are those where there is a reasonable likelihood that a failure of the ITGC process would result in a failure of critical IT functionality, or a change to data that leads to an undetected material misstatement.

- It is not necessary to test every ITGC control that relates to a significant application—only those that are required to address the ITGC process risks as explained above.

Additional details on how to perform this step can be found in the GAIT Methodology, which is strongly recommended. GAIT enables an organization not only to have an efficient Sarbanes-Oxley scope, but to identify the *right* ITGC key controls to rely on and test.

> **KEY POINT:**
> KEY ITGC CONTROLS
>
> It is not necessary to test every ITGC control that relates to a significant application—only those that are required to address the ITGC process risks.

4. Identify the ITGC to test that meet control objectives.

Key controls are identified to achieve each of the IT control objectives. That may require one or a combination of related key controls, which operate within ITGC processes.

It should be noted that, in some organizations, IT general control processes may reside outside the IT function even if nothing is outsourced. For example, some technology companies may delegate management of the security of part of the network to the product development function, and other companies may have management of data warehouses (including security and application change control) within the finance organization.

5. Perform a "reasonable person" review.

The identification of key controls within ITGC can be complex, especially the first time it is done. I recommend that management take the opportunity to step back and review the selection to determine whether a reasonable person, also known as a prudent official, would consider the selection of key controls to be appropriate.

This is also the time to determine whether there are any risks within IT general control processes that should be addressed because they affect multiple applications and their functionality. This *aggregation* effect is important. Many, but not all, IT general control processes relate to multiple applications. While a failure in an IT general control process might not represent a significant risk to an individual application and its critical functionality, the combined effect on multiple applications might be sufficient to justify testing related key controls.

4. *Indirect Controls*

Most of the discussion around what we are calling *indirect controls* (defined as controls required to address COSO principles that only have an *indirect* effect on the risk of material misstatement) has been around controls that operate at the entity-level.

The SEC guidance describes entity-level controls:

> "The term 'entity-level controls' ... describes aspects of a system of internal control that have a pervasive effect on the entity's system of internal control such as controls related to the control environment (for example, management's philosophy and operating style; integrity and ethical values; board or audit committee oversight; and assignment of authority and responsibility); controls over management override; the company's risk assessment process; centralized processing and controls, including shared service environments; controls to monitor results of operations; controls to monitor other controls, including activities of the internal audit function, the audit committee, and self-assessment programs; controls over

the period-end financial reporting process; and policies that address significant business control and risk management practices. The terms 'company-level' and 'entity-wide' are also commonly used to describe these controls."

In the paragraph above, the following generally have a *direct* relationship to the risk of financial misstatement: controls over management override; centralized processing and controls (e.g., at a shared services center); controls to monitor results of operations; many of the controls to monitor other controls; and controls over the period-end financial reporting process.

However, the following only have an *indirect* relationship: management's tone at the top; code of ethics; board or audit committee oversight; the risk management process; and the activities of the internal audit function. Weaknesses in indirect entity-level controls may indicate a higher risk that key controls will not operate effectively. They do not represent, by themselves, a direct risk of material misstatement. As explained earlier, these controls are required to address several COSO principles.

AS 5 echoes the concept that some controls have an *indirect* effect on the risk of a material misstatement:

> "Entity-level controls vary in nature and precision:
>
> - Some entity-level controls, such as certain control environment activities, have an important, but indirect, effect on the likelihood that a misstatement will be detected or prevented on a timely basis. These controls might affect the other controls the auditor selects for testing and the nature, timing, and extent of procedures the auditor performs on other controls.
>
> - Some entity-level controls monitor the effectiveness of other controls. Such controls might be designed to identify possible breakdowns in lower-level controls, but not at a level of precision that would, by themselves, sufficiently address the assessed risk that misstatements to a relevant assertion will be prevented or detected on a timely basis. These controls, when operating effectively, might allow the auditor to reduce the testing of other controls."

The indirect controls required to address COSO principles such as the integrity and competence of individuals performing or responsible for internal controls are not limited to the entity-level. For example, direct supervision and training performed within a unit may be relied upon for those principles and they operate at the local, business process, and unit level. Many organizations have a corporate-wide code of business conduct (i.e., an entity-level activity), but the code is translated into each local language and training and certification in the code is performed at the local level (i.e., at the activity level).

The external auditor is directed in AS 5 to review many of these indirect controls because weaknesses could indicate a greater *risk* that the key controls are ineffective:

> "The auditor must test those entity-level controls that are important to the auditor's conclusion about whether the company has effective internal control over financial reporting. The auditor's evaluation of entity-level controls can result in increasing or decreasing the testing that the auditor otherwise would have performed on other controls."

The PCAOB has not updated AS 5 to reflect the 2013 update of the COSO framework (in the opinion of the author it is likely to decide no update is required), but includes requirements for the external auditor that are not inconsistent with many of the COSO principles. With respect to the Control Environment, it says:

> "Because of its importance to effective internal control over financial reporting, the auditor must evaluate the control environment at the company. As part of evaluating the control environment, the auditor should assess:
>
> - Whether management's philosophy and operating style promote effective internal control over financial reporting;
>
> - Whether sound integrity and ethical values, particularly of top management, are developed and understood; and
>
> - Whether the Board or audit committee understands and exercises oversight responsibility over financial reporting and internal control."

The contrast between the PCAOB guidance and the guidance for management from the SEC (also not yet updated for COSO 2013) is significant. While the PCAOB spells out specific areas that must be addressed by the external auditor, the SEC guidance is more principles-based. It asks management to use the adopted internal controls framework (e.g., COSO) to determine how much work should be done on the indirect entity-level controls:

> "In addition to identifying controls that address the financial reporting risks of individual financial reporting elements, management also evaluates whether it has controls over the period-end financial reporting process, controls in place to address the entity-level and other pervasive elements of ICFR that its chosen control framework prescribes as necessary for an effective system of internal control. This would ordinarily include, for example, considering how and whether controls related to the control environment, controls over management override, the entity-level risk assessment process and monitoring activities, and the policies that address significant business control and risk management practices are adequate for purposes of an effective system of internal control. The control frameworks and related guidance may be useful tools for evaluating the adequacy of these elements of ICFR."

Note that the controls within the period-ending financial reporting process are generally direct controls that are separately identified by the top-down approach described earlier.

I agree with the principles of the SEC's guidance. Management should test those controls that are relevant to assessing that a reasonable system of internal control is in place. As indicated earlier, that includes the *direct* key controls relied upon to prevent or detect material misstatements together with the *indirect* key controls relied upon to provide assurance that the higher risk COSO principles are achieved.

One way of thinking about the distinction between direct and indirect controls is through the potential effect if there are weaknesses in each:

- A weakness in a *direct* key control implies that material errors may be introduced without timely detection.

- A weakness in an *indirect* key control implies that there is a higher likelihood that *direct* key controls will fail (for example, through management override or due to staff competence). The root cause of many failures in direct key controls lies in defects in indirect key controls.

The approach recommended here is to assess the risk presented should any of the COSO principles fail to be achieved. Where the risk is low, the assessment of internal control over financial reporting for Sarbanes-Oxley purposes may rely on management self-assessment. Where the risk is higher, indirect key controls should be identified and tested. Those indirect key controls and the testing performed should be sufficient to demonstrate that the risk of a material misstatement is low.

COSO emphasizes, appropriately, that management should exercise its judgment in deciding which principles are relevant to the assessment of internal control for any objective, including for Sarbanes-Oxley. However, it is prudent to assume (consistent with COSO statements) that all principles are relevant and need to be addressed. The level of work (i.e., the number of related key controls and the nature and extent of testing) can and should be adjusted based on risk.

As explained below, many of the principles do not have a *direct* effect on the likelihood of a material misstatement of the financials files with the SEC. Their effect is *indirect*: they affect the likelihood that the controls that have a more direct effect will fail. Therefore, the risk from a defect in achieving these principles is best assessed after understanding the population of direct key controls. The recommended process, accordingly, identifies key controls relating to these principles *after* financial reporting risks and the direct key controls have been identified. These key controls, which only have an indirect effect, are most often found at the entity-level and are referred to in this book as "indirect controls."

The process of defining the scope of work for Sarbanes-Oxley purposes is, as explained earlier, designed to be efficient and focused only on areas where there is at least a reasonable possibility of a material weakness. Management may decide to perform more work than is strictly required because of a desire (for example by the audit committee or executive management) for a greater level of assurance.

The recommended process is to obtain a self-assessment from management (which may be prepared on its behalf by management of the Sarbanes-Oxley program) for each of the COSO principles. Where they are known (typically because they were included in the scope of work for the prior year's Sarbanes-Oxley assessment), it is useful to reference the key controls that support the assessment. COSO has provided a template that organizations might find useful as a basis for the self-assessment. While it is generalized and not specific to Sarbanes-Oxley assessments, it should be relatively easy to adapt it for that use.

The discussion that follows explains for each principle how much reliance will generally be placed on management's self-assessment. Consistent with regulatory guidance, reliance will typically only be placed where the risk from a defect relating to the principle is low. Otherwise, key controls will be identified and included in the scope of testing.

Control Environment Principles

1. The organization demonstrates a commitment to integrity and ethical values.

This is certainly a very important attribute of any organization and its overall system of internal control, typically acknowledged as such by the board and senior management. The root cause of many highly-publicized internal control failures have been failures in this area.

However, the activities involved in addressing the principle (such as the establishment, communication, and training of employees in a Code of Conduct) are *indirect entity-level controls*. They do not have a direct effect on the level of risk to the financial statements. Instead, they have an indirect effect: when an organization does not demonstrate a commitment to integrity there is a greater level of risk that the *direct* key controls (i.e., the combination of controls relied upon to detect or prevent a material misstatement, including financial statement fraud) will not be properly performed on a regular basis.

It is important to recognize that the application of this principle to internal control over financial reporting relates *primarily* to the integrity of those involved in preparing, reviewing, and approving the financial statements, and the likelihood that they would deliberately introduce or fail to prevent materially incorrect entries. For example, the presence of higher levels than acceptable of theft (such as in a retail business) is not necessarily an indication of higher levels of risk to financial reporting.

Management should use its judgment to determine how wide to spread the application of this principle. In some cases, it may be prudent to include senior management that are not involved in performing or overseeing the performance of controls over financial reporting, because they might still be able to influence the actions of those that are involved.

While the principle relates to indirect entity-level controls, it is important to recognize that the root cause of most corporate failures, financial statement frauds, and even of individual control failures has been either the integrity and/or competence of people (principle 4). Therefore, even though related controls are indirect, they are not of secondary importance.

Management should use its judgment in applying this principle as part of its assessment of internal control over financial reporting.

Because this area is the most common root cause of material financial statement fraud, it is prudent to consider it a high-risk area and related key indirect entity-level controls should be included in scope and tested. (Note that if there are strong controls within the Monitoring component they may provide a high level of assurance of the proper operation of direct key controls and at least mitigate any deficiency in this area.)

When assessing whether a principle is high or low risk, we recommend asking this question: Would a defect in the presence or functioning of this principle indicate that there is at least a reasonable possibility of a material misstatement of the financial statements filed with the SEC? Where the principle only has an indirect effect on financial statement risk, does it indicate at least a reasonable possibility that direct key controls relied upon to either prevent or detect material errors would fail?

Assessment of this principle will be based on management's self-assessment together with the results of testing related indirect key controls.

2. **The board of directors demonstrates independence from management and exercises oversight of the development and performance of internal control.**

This is another desirable principle as part of the overall system of internal control, and again the activities addressing it are *indirect entity-level controls.*

However, the actions of the board are remote from the operation of the direct controls relied upon to prevent or detect material misstatement of the financials. It is rare for a member of the board to be the first to detect a material error, and even rarer for the organization to rely on the board to detect such an error.

On the other hand, a demonstrably weak board or one that does not contain sufficient expertise to oversee internal controls over financial reporting, the performance of the internal and external auditors, or the identification and management of risk, is likely—over time—to fail to recognize deficiencies in such matters as integrity and competence.

Judgment should be applied by management in determining whether this principle should be assessed as high risk (requiring the identification and testing of indirect entity-level controls) or low risk, when reliance may be placed on management self-assessments. (Note that in general only an egregious failure—such as the failure to ensure the appointment of a qualified chief financial officer—is likely to result in a material weakness in the system of internal control over financial reporting.)

The principle will be assessed based on management's self-assessment together with the results of testing of related key indirect controls, if any have been identified to address high-risk areas.

3. Management establishes, with board oversight, structures, reporting lines, and appropriate authorities and responsibilities in the pursuit of objectives.

Another set of indirect entity-level controls, this principle should be assessed with respect to the people responsible for the operation of internal control over financial reporting.

The most likely issue to arise from this principle and its potential to adversely affect the system of internal control over financial reporting relates to the reporting lines of those responsible for such activities as approving journal entries and ensuring compliance with applicable accounting and reporting standards. If key individuals in these processes do not report independently of operating management (for example, if they report to a business unit manager), they may be subject to undue influence that affects the integrity of their actions, creating a higher risk to the operation of related direct key controls.

The effect of any issue around this principle cannot be assessed until the combination of *direct* key controls has been identified. At that point, it is useful to step back, consider the full set of key controls, and assess whether any failure with respect to satisfying this principle has a significant effect on the risk that the direct key controls may not operate reliably and effectively. (Note: do not forget to include in this assessment those responsible for key IT general controls.)

The level of risk should be used to determine the level of work that should be performed to confirm any management self-assessment of this principle.

The principle will be assessed based on management's self-assessment and the results of testing of any indirect key controls.

4. The organization demonstrates a commitment to attract, develop, and retain competent individuals in alignment with objectives.

The reliable operation of key controls over financial reporting is at risk unless the people performing them are competent. This principle relates to a set of indirect entity-level controls (which may operate at multiple levels within the organization, such as at the corporate headquarters, a business unit, a division, or an individual location).

As noted above, the root cause of most control failures is people and their integrity and/or competence. Therefore, it is prudent to assess this principle as high risk and key indirect entity-level controls identified and included in the scope of testing.

While it is possible to assess controls in general within human resource processes, the more practical approach when assessing internal control over financial reporting (remembering that the assessment is as of a point in time) is to refine the assessment to address the competence of only those individuals currently performing key controls. For example, the *retention* of competent individuals is unlikely to be a risk to the integrity of the financial statements unless a competent person is replaced by somebody who is not competent.

Management should use its judgment in determining the level of work to be performed in identifying and assessing controls over the competence of those involved in the operation of key controls. If turnover among these individuals is low, it may be more appropriate to consider the competence of each of the individuals when assessing and testing each key control. However, if there is a significant level of turnover, the human resources processes involved in hiring and other activities becomes more important and may require assessment and testing. Note that it is important to extend this assessment to all key controls, including any indirect entity-level key controls.

This principle will be assessed based on management's self-assessment of any low risk areas together with the results of testing of (a) identified key indirect controls, and (b) direct key controls where the competence of the individuals performing the controls is included in the test.

5. **The organization holds individuals accountable for their internal control responsibilities in the pursuit of objectives.**

This is another principle that is important in general but typically remote from the operation of internal control over financial reporting. It is not as if there are, as discussed in the COSO framework, "performance measures, incentives, and rewards" for materially correct financial reporting. However, there may be issues if, similar to the point in principle 3, there is undue influence to meet financial targets or otherwise induce inappropriate failures to prevent or detect material misstatements.

On the other hand, when the CFO and other top management fail to hold individuals responsible for control failures, the likelihood of control failures occurring and persisting is higher.

Absent evidence of an issue relating to this principle (such as evidence of management complacency when there are control failures), management might consider this a low risk and rely on management self-assessment.

Risk Assessment Principles

6. **The organization specifies objectives with sufficient clarity to enable the identification and assessment of risks relating to objectives.**

In general, risk is assessed relative to its potential effect on the achievement of objectives. That holds equally true for risks related to financial reporting. However, the objectives are already determined by regulations and regulatory guidance and no work will be required in assessing this principle. It will generally be assessed as achieved.

7. **The organization identifies risks to the achievement of its objectives across the entity and analyzes risks as a basis for determining how the risks should be managed.**

The risk of a material omission, misstatement, or other error in the financial statement is at the heart of the assessment of internal control over financial reporting. Risks should be identified and assessed using a top-down approach, as described in this book.

It is general practice for those responsible for assessing internal control over financial reporting to perform the risk assessment, so it would be unusual to see much testing being performed for this principle. The principle will typically be assessed as achieved if a top-down and risk-based approach, as discussed here, is followed.

8. **The organization considers the potential for fraud in assessing risks to the achievement of objectives.**

The likelihood of fraud that results in a material error in the financials should be included in the risk assessment in principle 7. COSO identifies this as a separate principle to emphasize the importance of considering fraud risk.

The principle will generally be considered as achieved if the consideration of fraud risk is included in the top-down and risk-based scoping process.

9. The organization identifies and assesses changes that could significantly impact the system of internal control.

Again, this is a normal part of the risk assessment in principle 7. It is important that the risk assessment be updated through the year.

The principle will normally be considered achieved if the risk assessments in principle 7 and 8 are updated through the year in response to changes in the business, accounting regulations, etc.

Control Activities Principles

10. The organization selects and develops control activities that contribute to the mitigation of risks to the achievement of objectives to acceptable levels.

Once the risks have been identified (principle 7), the key controls relied upon to prevent or detect material errors are identified. These direct key controls are generally found in the Control Activity component.

While the text of the principle states that these "contribute to the mitigation of risks to the achievement of objectives to acceptable levels," the system of internal control should provide reasonable assurance that they ensure risks are at acceptable levels. Note that the regulators have defined "reasonable assurance" and "acceptable levels" based on whether there is a reasonable likelihood of a material error.

The assessment of this principle should be based on whether testing of key controls confirms that the design and operation of the system of internal control provides that reasonable assurance.

11. The organization selects and develops general control activities over technology to support the achievement of objectives.

Key IT General Controls are part of the combination of key controls relied upon to prevent or detect material misstatements. The identification of key IT general controls should be performed by extending the top-down and risk-based approach to identifying key controls within business processes (including entity-level controls). Key IT general controls provide reasonable assurance that key automated controls (including security) perform consistently as desired.

The assessment of this principle should generally be included in the assessment of principle 10. COSO identifies this as a separate principle to emphasize the dependence of organizations on the effective and reliable use of technology.

12. The organization deploys control activities through policies that establish what is expected and procedures that put policies into action.

The continued and reliable performance of controls is enhanced when the procedures involved are well-documented, known by the individuals who perform the controls, and maintained as systems and processes change. However, experience has shown that controls may be reliably performed by experienced individuals without reference to out-of-date documentation. There is no *direct* relationship between the quality of controls documentation and the quality of controls execution. However, when there is a high degree of turnover among those responsible for controls, the risk that controls may not be executed flawlessly increases when the related documentation and training of new employees is flawed.

Documentation of accounting policies and related standards and procedures is important. When these do not reflect current regulatory and other requirements, or are not properly communicated across the organization to everyone who should adhere to them, the risk that material errors will be introduced into the financial statements increases.

The COSO framework acknowledges that policies and procedures may be communicated orally and that may be sufficient. However, management should use its judgment to assess whether risks related to this principle, either relative to controls documentation or to accounting standards, is high. Where the risk is high, such that a defect makes it more than reasonably likely that direct controls will not prevent or detect material errors in the financials, related *indirect key controls* should be identified and included in the scope.

It is prudent to assess risks relating to documentation and communication of accounting standards as high.

With respect to controls documentation, in practice this may be best assessed when considering the design and operation of each key control—direct and indirect.

With respect to policies and other documentation, the assessment will typically be based on management self-assessment together with the results of testing on related indirect key controls.

Information and Communication Principles

13. The organization obtains or generates and uses relevant, quality information to support the functioning of internal control.

The operation of many key controls is dependent upon the quality of the information available to the individuals performing them. This would normally be addressed as part of the testing of those key controls: is sufficient information available when the control is performed? A separate set of testing for this principle should, therefore, not be necessary.

This principle will generally be assessed based on the results of testing of individual key controls, both direct and indirect.

14. The organization internally communicates information, including objectives and responsibilities for internal control, necessary to support the functioning of internal control.

As with principle 13, this will normally be assessed as part of the testing of each key control.

15. The organization communicates with external parties regarding matters affecting the functioning of internal control.

The framework discusses communications from external parties, such as from auditors at service organizations. These may be relied upon to address risks relating to activities at those service organizations, when the reviews of such communications become key controls. It is unlikely that separate testing of controls related to this principle will be necessary because reliance on third parties should be identified in the risk assessment process and appropriate key controls should be in place and tested.

This principle will be assessed based on the results of testing of key controls around service organizations.

Monitoring Activities Principles

16. The organization selects, develops, and performs ongoing and/or separate evaluations to ascertain whether the components of internal control are present and functioning.

The annual assessment by management of the system of internal control over financial reporting satisfies this principle.

However, it should be noted that where management has ongoing monitoring of controls in place (and they are assessed and tested as key controls), it may mitigate deficiencies related to the operation of the direct key controls themselves. For example, if there is continuous monitoring of the operation of key controls related to bank reconciliations, it is likely to compensate for concerns related to the experience of the individuals or the documentation of the control procedures.

17. The organization evaluates and communicates internal control deficiencies in a timely manner to those parties responsible for taking corrective action, including senior management and the board of directors, as appropriate.

An argument can be made that this speaks to "tone at the top" and could have been included in the Control Environment component. The principle is relevant, as a set of indirect controls, because a failure to take corrective action not only means that controls continue to be weak, but there may be a lack of proper focus and importance given to the system of internal control.

Assessment can be made by reference to the timeliness of correction of deficiencies in key controls, which is easily tested.

The last step (f) involves stepping back and considering the entire set of key controls, both direct and indirect, within business processes and IT general control processes, and confirming that they should provide the level of reasonable assurance that is desired.

Management Self-Assessment of COSO Principles

Because management is required to perform the Sarbanes-Oxley assessment based on a recognized internal controls framework, and only the COSO framework has been recognized by the SEC, it is prudent to complete a formal assessment of all 17 principles in the 2013 COSO internal control framework.

The recommended approach, as discussed earlier, is to ask senior management to perform a formal self-assessment for each of the principles. For low-risk principles, the Sarbanes-Oxley scope can rely on the self-assessment. For high-risk principles, the assessment is supplemented by related key controls.

COSO has provided *Illustrative Tools for Assessing Effectiveness of a System of Internal Control—Templates*; section 2, "Component Evaluation" is the one I would use as a basis for the self-assessment form. I recommend that the form be modified to meet the organization's specific needs and include:

- Sufficient explanation of each principle, either within the document or referenced from the document, to enable management to complete the self-assessment.

- An evaluation that states whether management believes that the principle is "present and functioning" (i.e., the system of internal control is not only designed to achieve the principle but is currently doing so).

- The identification of any related controls that support the self-assessment.

- The identification of any known deficiencies. However, I would assess them as described in the section on deficiency assessment later in the book.

- An assessment as to whether this principle is low or high risk, as explained previously. Prudence dictates that the principles related to integrity and competence be rated high.

- For those principles assessed as high risk, which related controls will be identified as key controls and included in scope.

The Component Evaluation form includes a section at the end of each section for evaluating each component based on the assessments for each related principle. I prefer not to use this, but to consider and assess all deficiencies as described in that section of this book.

Each principle was discussed in some detail earlier, and more can be found in the COSO framework documents.

Management is not really in a position to objectively assess its own philosophy and operating style, or the operations of the board or its committees. One path is for management to request that internal audit include assessments of related governance processes in its periodic audit plan.

The external auditor may be able to rely on portions of management's testing on these entity-level controls, so coordination to synchronize approaches and scope will be of value. This should especially be encouraged when internal audit includes aspects of governance processes in its audit plan.

5. *Spreadsheets, Models, and Similar Issues*

Much has been made about the risks to financial reporting through errors in spreadsheets and user computing in general, including the use of Microsoft Access databases and similar tools (collectively referred to as "spreadsheets" for convenience here). Because spreadsheet errors have been found at a number of companies that resulted in material errors in their financial statements, this risk should be acknowledged and addressed. However, it is also important to ensure that the Sarbanes-Oxley program remains focused on the risk of material misstatement—and focuses, therefore, on those spreadsheets used in key controls (or other critical IT functionality, as discussed above) where an error could lead to an undetected material error in the financials.

Risks related to spreadsheets include:

1. Errors in the download from the company's enterprise application systems, such as:

    a. An incomplete download (e.g., missing a G/L or a region).

    b. An out-of-date download.

    c. A partial download, where transmission or other errors prevented completion of the entire download.

    d. Use of an intermediate database (e.g., a data warehouse) that is not complete, accurate, or current. See the next section for specific discussion of data warehouses.

    e. The incorrect population of the downloaded data into the various cells in the spreadsheet.

2. Errors in spreadsheet calculations, sorts, or other programmable elements.

3. Use of an out-of-date spreadsheet, including use of a current spreadsheet where the calculations are not refreshed.

4. Changes to the data by the user.

5. Errors in the understanding or use of the spreadsheet (e.g., where the user is not the developer and picks up the wrong total).

6. Changes to the spreadsheet by another user due to poor security controls.

Where errors in spreadsheets could result in the failure of a key controls and an undetected material misstatement, the risk needs to be addressed by key controls.

Some consultants have advised the use of specialized software to manage the risk of spreadsheet error, and there are many products of value. However, before acquiring and implementing additional products at a significant cost, it is recommended that management consider the following approach. It will help identify the risks that should be addressed.

- When a key business control includes the use of a spreadsheet, determine whether an undetected error in the spreadsheet could cause the control to fail and result in a material error in the financial statements. Also, determine whether the spreadsheet is essential to the key control (e.g., enabling a review of an estimate) or incidental (e.g., used to list the documents being reviewed).

- Will the normal operation of the control detect an error in the spreadsheet? There are two ways this can happen:

  - If the spreadsheet is used in a reconciliation process. For example, if original documents are summarized in a spreadsheet and compared to the updated general ledger balance, an error in the spreadsheet will result in an out-of-balance condition with the general ledger.

  - The control includes user procedures to confirm the completeness and accuracy of the spreadsheet. For example, if a spreadsheet is used to analyze sales invoices by region, then confirmation of the totals to the general ledger will ensure that the download of data into the spreadsheet is complete and formulas are properly calculating the totals.

- If an error in the spreadsheet would not be detected in the normal operation of the control, understand the specific nature of the risk and take action accordingly:

  - If the risk is in the download from the general ledger (or other computer system) directly into the spreadsheet, consider changing the design of the download process to include a user control (e.g., a user verification of the spreadsheet totals to the general ledger).

  - If the risk is around the download of information into a data warehouse or similar, consider adding controls over the download and ensuring that the spreadsheet is balanced back to the data warehouse.

- If the risk is that the spreadsheet uses data from a data warehouse that may be incomplete, out of date, or otherwise unreliable, consider adding controls over the data warehouse.

- If the issue is that the user is entering data into the spreadsheet manually, consider adding a control to validate the completeness and accuracy of the data in the spreadsheet.

- If the risk of error is in the calculations, consider whether the user can review the results in such a way that it will confirm the calculations are correct. If the calculations are too complex for a review, consider replacing the spreadsheet with a report or other program developed and maintained by IT. A risk of using complex calculations in a spreadsheet is that the user may inadvertently introduce a mistake into the spreadsheet. Converting the spreadsheet into a report developed and maintained by IT will provide greater assurance that the calculations will continue to function properly, with all changes to the calculations tested and approved, assuming that IT has adequate IT general controls over those reports.

- If there is no alternative to relying on the spreadsheet and its calculations, there are two options. Management can decide to perform independent testing of the spreadsheet (in the same way it can test automated controls). Alternatively, it can identify key controls that address each of the identified risks. (The decision may be to rely on key controls for some spreadsheets and independently test others). For example, it may be necessary to identify key controls over:

> **KEY POINTS:**
> SPREADSHEETS
>
> ► If an error in the spreadsheet would not be detected in the normal operation of the control, understand where the risk is and take action accordingly.
>
> ► If a walk-through or other formal assessment of the control design is performed, it should include a discussion of how the completeness and accuracy of the spreadsheet results are assured.

- The validity of changes to the spreadsheet, including testing and approval.

- Input, whether automated or manual, of data into the spreadsheet.

- The security of the spreadsheet so that only valid, tested, and approved changes are made and that data is not inappropriately changed.

- The way in which the spreadsheet is used and the results are interpreted. For example, there should be controls to ensure that all data is input and validated before the results of the spreadsheet are used in the key controls. In addition, there should be assurance (e.g., through documentation or user instructions) that the use of the spreadsheet is correct (e.g., the correct totals are used). An example of the latter is where a spreadsheet has multiple analyses of the data; the user should understand which analysis and which totals should be used.

  - The key controls over spreadsheet risks should be included in the inventory of key controls subject to assessment and testing.

To assist the external auditor's review, and to serve as a solid double check in this area, management should consider developing an inventory of all spreadsheets that are a significant part of a key control or a critical part of the financial reporting process. The inventory should describe how assurance is obtained for completeness and accuracy and other spreadsheet risks, including which key controls are relied on for that purpose.

From the point of view of efficiency and risk reduction, management should give continuing consideration to replacing spreadsheets with more reliable enterprise applications, such as business intelligence (discussed in the next section), financial close applications, or similar.

Similar risks exist when companies use sophisticated models for complex calculations (such as for reserves). While these models may have been built in MS-Excel and essentially covered by the discussion above, they may also have been developed in specialized software[15] or use third-party applications. The key is to identify financial reporting risks from the use of the models, such as where errors in how the models work or the integrity of the data input could result in a failure of key controls and a material misstatement. The process described above can be followed, with questions about spreadsheets replaced by questions about models. Management should consider placing models, especially where they use specialized applications, under the control of the IT function and covered by their IT general controls.

6. *Data Warehouses and Business Intelligence*

Special attention should be paid when hybrid key controls use reports from a data warehouse, also referred to sometimes as a data store, repository, or similar. The term "business intelligence" refers to the entire process of extracting data from enterprise applications, storing that data in data warehouses, and analyzing the data and delivering information to the user in the form of reports or on the screen. In addition, such reports may be used in business processes (for example, as a basis for a journal entry to update a reserve account).

Where reliance is being placed, as a form of critical IT functionality, on information from a data warehouse, additional risks may be introduced that require attention from appropriate key controls. Note that the following risks would only be relevant to the extent that they relate to key controls or critical IT functionality (also noting that the latter is not limited to activities of the IT department).

- Data from the enterprise applications may not be completely downloaded.

- Errors may be introduced in the downloads, especially when potentially inconsistent data is downloaded from multiple applications and combined in the data warehouse.

- Downloads may not be current.

- Access to the data warehouse may not be secure, with a risk that the data is inappropriately changed.

- Inappropriate changes may be made by individuals with approved access to the data.

- The data may be defined, such as through the use of data universes, incorrectly. Without getting into technical details, data in the warehouses is described in a universe. Programs that analyze the data use these universes to extract the appropriate data, so if the universe is incorrect, the extract and analysis will be wrong.

- The programs used to generate the report (or information on screen) may not function as intended (just as enterprise application code may not function as intended) due to deficiencies in the development, maintenance, or security of the programs.

- Parameters used to run the analysis may be out of date or otherwise incorrect.

In many cases, business intelligence is not owned and operated by IT in the same way as enterprise applications such as general ledger or accounts payable. The analytical routines (programs) are frequently written and maintained by users who may also maintain the data universes and even have the data warehouse on their own servers, outside the direct control of IT. When reviewing the risks and identifying controls related to data warehouses, consideration should be given to.

- Who owns and operates the data extract? Is it IT (which is more reliable) or the user (generally less reliable)?

- Who owns and is responsible for the data warehouse? Is it IT?

- Who developed and maintains the data universe and the programs used for the analysis? Again, is it IT?

- Are there business process key controls over the integrity of the data used in the analysis? Are they sufficient to identify any error that could lead to a failure of a key hybrid control or result in a material misstatement (such as the posting of an incorrect journal entry for a reserve account)?

- Are there ITGC that can be relied upon to address risks related to data warehouses?

As a general rule, there is a lower level of risk when IT is responsible for business intelligence. From a design point of view, management should consider putting all aspects of business intelligence (such as maintenance of the data warehouse and reports) that represent a potential risk to financial reporting under IT control.

7. *Controls Performed by Third-Party Organizations*

Many companies have achieved cost savings or other benefits by outsourcing selected functions, such as payroll processing, processing of stock options, or data center management. Management needs to consider these outsourced operations when developing the scope of the Sarbanes-Oxley assessment.[16] If key controls are operated by third-party organizations, they should be assessed and tested before management can be assured that the controls are adequately designed and operating effectively.

One approach is to treat processes and related controls at a third-party organization in the same way as management addresses processes and controls within the organization. Management needs to ensure the processes are adequately documented, identify and assess the adequacy of the design of key controls, and perform tests to confirm the controls are operating effectively and are consistent with the documentation. Management may find that the service provider has good documentation, in which case it need not duplicate that effort, even if the provider's documentation is not in the same format or style as that used by the company. Management may also be able to place some degree of reliance on any testing by the provider of its internal controls. However, management needs to consider not only the competence of the personnel performing such testing but also the independence of the personnel from the provider's management.

> **KEY POINT:**
> CONTROLS AT SERVICE ORGANIZATIONS
>
> If key controls are operated by third-party organizations, they should be assessed and tested.

Management may decide to design the system of internal controls so that controls operated within the company can be relied upon. While this may appear, and often is, inefficient duplication of the service provider's procedures, it reduces the risk that the latter might fail. I suggest looking for ways that errors at the service provider that could result in a material misstatement might be detected within a reasonable time. In other words, rather than duplicate detailed transaction-level controls, where practical, look for detective, direct entity-level controls.

It is important to consider Sarbanes-Oxley requirements as part of contracting with service vendors. Questions that might be addressed include:

- Is there an obligation for the vendor to have adequate controls for Sarbanes-Oxley purposes, meeting defined control objectives agreed to by management?

- Does management have an opportunity to evaluate the design of those controls?

- What recourse will the company have should the controls at the service provider fail?

- Is there an obligation for the service provider to correct any deficiencies, and in what period of time?

- How promptly should the service provider notify the company if a control failure is suspected?

- Will the company have the right to audit the key controls for Sarbanes-Oxley?

- Will the service provider allow testing by the company's external auditor?

- Will the service provider provide an SSAE 16/SOC 1 report (see below) or equivalent?

Most service providers, especially in the United States but an increasing number globally, recognize their customers' have to obtain assurance over their provider's controls. Rather than have every customer send a team of auditors to document and test their controls, these providers engage a third-party auditor to perform an attest engagement. Until 2011, these engagements were performed under the AICPA's Statement of Auditing Standards Number 70 (SAS 70), which defined how independent auditors identify the controls to test, perform testing of the controls, and report the results.

SAS 70 has been replaced by the AICPA's Statement on Standards for Attestation Engagements No.16 (SSAE 16), *Reporting on Controls at a Service Organization*. SSAE 16 is almost identical to a new standard from the International Auditing and Assurance Standards Board (IAASB): the International Standard on Assurance Engagements (ISAE) 3402, *Assurance Report on Controls at a Service Organization*. (Standard-setting organizations in a number of countries have similar attest standards, such as the Canadian Institute of Chartered Accountants' Handbook Section 5970, the U.K. Audit and Assurance Faculty Standard 01/06, Germany's IDW PS 951, and Japan's Audit Standards Committee Report No. 18.)

Reports from audits performed by independent audit firms in accordance with SSAE 16, ISAE 3402, or equivalent can be relied upon by management as assurance that the providers' controls are adequate under certain conditions:

a) Management needs to identify the key controls it relies on the provider to perform; review the report, which should contain a description of the key controls tested; and confirm that the design of the control is sufficient to meet management's control objectives.

b) The company typically will need controls that work with those at the service provider. For example, the company should have controls to ensure all transactions are transmitted to the provider for processing. Management should ensure these controls work effectively in combination with the provider's controls. SSAE 16 reports should include a description of the controls the provider expects its customers to have. This is a section that management should review carefully but not rely only upon what the provider says. Management should determine the key controls it needs based on its own understanding of the processes and controls at the service provider and within the company.

c) Management should review the report with care to ensure the testing is sufficient to confirm the adequacy of the controls it will rely on and then assess the results reported.

If the SSAE 16/SOC 1 (Service Organization Controls) report identifies deficiencies, management needs to determine what impact, if any, the deficiencies have on the key controls it relies on at the provider. For example, the report may identify deficiencies in Windows NT servers at an outsourced data center, while the company's software runs only on UNIX servers. Management may also find that controls within the company compensate or, at least, mitigate the deficiencies.

Service providers do not always provide assurance that any deficiencies will be corrected and retested before the end of their customer's fiscal year. While I believe management should work with the provider to include a commitment to address deficiencies in the contract, the provider may not be responsive. Therefore, management should ensure excellent communications are in place to provide as much notice as possible of potential audit issues.

Additional information on a SSAE 16/SOC 1 or ISSAE 3402 report can be obtained from the external auditor.

J. Fraud Risk Assessment

The concept of a fraud risk assessment is one that has been frequently misunderstood, even though PCAOB AS 2 clearly stated:

> "The auditor should evaluate all controls specifically intended to address the risks of fraud that have at least a reasonably possible likelihood of having a material effect on the company's financial statements."[17, 18]

AS 5 contains similar language:

> "...the auditor should evaluate whether the company's controls sufficiently address identified risks of material misstatement due to fraud."

The COSO 2013 framework as a separate principle for fraud risk: "Principle 8: The organization considers the potential for fraud in assessing risks to the achievement of objectives." COSO refers to fraudulent financial reporting in language consistent with the above. It is:

> "An intentional act designed to deceive users of external financial reports and that may result in a material omission from or misstatement of such financial reports."

The key to an efficient consideration of fraud is to focus on fraud schemes that could result in a _material_ misstatement of the financials.[19] Many thefts and frauds, while significant and important to prevent or at least detect promptly, are unlikely to result in a material error in the financial statements.

For example:

- The theft of inventory at a company that conducts a full physical inventory at year-end would not result in an error in the year-end financials because a write-off will have been taken.

- The approval and payment of duplicate or excessive payments for services are recorded correctly in the financial statements. The financials correctly reflect the amounts paid, on the appropriate line of the P&L, even if the amounts were paid twice.

There are a number of detailed guides, including those from The IIA[20] and each of the major accounting firms, on how to address fraud risk. The high-level approach is to:

- Identify the fraud schemes applicable to the company that might result in a material error in the financials if undetected. Particular attention should be given to schemes involving the management override of controls, including the approval and processing of manual journal entries.

- Identify the key controls that would either prevent or timely detect any such fraudulent activity, and confirm the adequacy of their design.

- Ensure that the identified key controls are tested.

One area of focus relates to restricted access (RA) and segregation of duties (SOD). As discussed earlier in section (a), it is possible to spend a significant amount of time assessing and testing these areas, because many frauds are the result of inappropriate access and especially a combination of access capabilities (e.g., the ability to both set up a vendor and approve invoices). In addition, there are significant business reasons (including the loss of assets) for ensuring appropriate RA and SOD are in place. The key to efficient Sarbanes-Oxley testing for RA and SOD is carefully focusing on access abilities where a resulting fraud could mean the financials are materially misstated. If management desires, additional RA and SOD testing for purely business risk management purposes may be added to Sarbanes-Oxley testing because the added cost of additional testing may be minimal. However, these non-Sarbanes-Oxley tests should be clearly identified as such to the external auditor.

K. Process and Control Documentation

The key business processes and, especially, the material transactions and related controls should be documented. There are various techniques and documentation styles for completing the documentation. However, management needs to complete documentation that:

- Enables a reasonably knowledgeable individual to understand the process. This person does not have to be an expert with experience in the area, but should have some knowledge of the company or its business. (This is also useful for training new staff and reduces the risk that they will not perform the key controls correctly.)

- Provides context for the key controls so that a reasonable person would understand their function.

- Details the operation of key controls, such as identifying who is performing the control, when the control is operating and at what frequency, how the control is performed, what evidence exists that the control was performed, and which reports are used in the operation of the control. It is valuable to agree with the external auditor on the quality standards to be established for control documentation.

- Overall, enables a reasonable person to have a basis upon which to assess the design of the controls. Are the controls identified and documented sufficiently to either prevent or detect a material misstatement?

It is critical to establish a change management process to ensure that documentation is kept up to date as processes and controls change. The business does not stop just because of Sarbanes-Oxley requirements. A sound change management process for Sarbanes-Oxley will likely have the following attributes:

- The process is well known to all business process owners.

> **KEY POINT:**
> CHANGE MANAGEMENT
>
> It is critical to establish a change management process to ensure that documentation is kept up to date as processes and controls change. The business does not stop just because of Sarbanes-Oxley requirements.

- Changes to business processes, including computer systems, are identified and the documentation is updated promptly.

- Changes to key controls are identified and assessed promptly to ensure the potential impact on Sarbanes-Oxley assessment and testing is understood.

- Planned changes, especially those planned for late in the fiscal year, are discussed to ensure the impact on the Sarbanes-Oxley assessment is understood. Serious consideration is given to delaying the change until after year-end.

The discussion above relates to requirements for effective and efficient scoping and testing. However, the quality of controls documentation can also be useful in addressing COSO principle 12: "The organization deploys control activities through policies that establish what is expected and procedures that put policies into action."

TESTING KEY CONTROLS

THE SEC's GUIDANCE includes an excellent discussion of how to obtain and evaluate evidence that the key controls, and therefore the system of internal control, are operating effectively. Their main points, with added commentary, are:

- "The evaluation of the operating effectiveness of a control considers whether the control is operating as designed and whether the person performing the control possesses the necessary authority and competence to perform the control effectively."

  Comment: It is important that management first confirm that key controls are effectively designed. That means that, assuming they operate as designed, the key controls will be effective in managing the identified risks to the financial statements. Assessment of the design is normally first done when the control is documented and identified as a key control; it is confirmed during a walkthrough (if one is performed—discussed further below). Testing of a key control will normally include (a) confirming the design of the control and (b) then testing to obtain evidence that it is performed as designed.

- "The evaluation procedures that management uses to gather evidence about the operation of the controls it identifies as adequately addressing the financial reporting risks for financial reporting elements should be tailored to management's assessment of the risk characteristics of both the individual financial reporting elements and the related controls."

  Comment: Two separate assessments of *risk* are recommended:

  - The risk of a material *misstatement* arising from the transactions and accounts affected by the control being tested. For example, the higher the balances, the more complex the accounting, the higher the fraud risk, and the greater the judgment being exercised, the greater the risk.

- The risk that the *controls* may not operate as designed. Factors affecting this risk might include the complexity of the control, the experience level of the individuals performing it, the level of judgment involved, whether the control has failed in prior period testing, the risk of management override, the nature of the control (e.g., manual or automated), and whether there are deficiencies in the context within which the control operates (i.e., deficiencies in any COSO principles).

The combined effect of these two risks is considered *ICFR risk*.

- "Management should ordinarily focus its evaluation of the operation of controls on areas posing the highest ICFR risk. Management's assessment of ICFR risk also considers the impact of entity-level controls, such as the relative strengths and weaknesses of the control environment, which may influence management's judgments about the risks of failure for particular controls."

  Comment: When the SEC is talking about the "control environment," it is referring to the COSO component by that name. It includes activities that by their nature are *indirect* controls. When these indirect controls are weak, they may indicate a higher risk that the operation of key controls will be inconsistent or ineffective.

- "Evidence about the effective operation of controls may be obtained from direct testing of controls and ongoing monitoring activities. The nature, timing, and extent of evaluation procedures necessary for management to obtain sufficient evidence of the effective operation of a control depend on the assessed ICFR risk."

  Comment: Monitoring activities relate to activities in the Monitoring component of the COSO internal control framework, as discussed earlier. They may include controls to monitor results of operations and controls to monitor other controls, including activities of the internal audit activity, the audit committee, and self-assessment programs. Where they provide sufficient evidence of the operation of key controls, they represent direct entity-level controls and in the top-down approach discussed above would probably be included as key controls to test.

- "In determining whether the evidence obtained is sufficient to provide a reasonable basis for its evaluation of the operation of ICFR, management should consider not only the quantity of evidence (for example, sample size) but also the qualitative characteristics of the evidence. The qualitative characteristics of the evidence include the nature of the evaluation procedures performed, the period of time to which the evidence relates, the objectivity of those evaluating the controls, and, in the case of ongoing monitoring activities, the extent of validation through direct testing of underlying controls."

Comment: This guide does not include recommendations for test sample sizes. Instead, I recommend that management adopt the guidelines followed by its external auditor. Those are generally based on sound statistical theory, and following them will increase the likelihood that the auditor will be able to place reliance on management's testing.

- "For any individual control, different combinations of the nature, timing, and extent of evaluation procedures may provide sufficient evidence. The sufficiency of evidence is not necessarily determined by any of these attributes individually."

- "In smaller companies, management's daily interaction with its controls may provide it with sufficient knowledge about their operation to evaluate the operation of ICFR. Knowledge from daily interaction includes information obtained by ongoing direct involvement with and direct supervision of the execution of the control by those responsible for the assessment of the effectiveness of ICFR.

"Management should consider its particular facts and circumstances when determining whether its daily interaction with controls provides sufficient evidence to evaluate the operating effectiveness of ICFR. For example, daily interaction may be sufficient when the operation of controls is centralized and the number of personnel involved is limited. Conversely, daily interaction in companies with multiple management reporting layers or operating segments would generally not provide sufficient evidence, because those responsible for assessing the effectiveness of ICFR would not ordinarily be sufficiently knowledgeable about the operation of the controls. In these situations, management would ordinarily use direct testing or ongoing monitoring-type evaluation procedures to obtain reasonable support for the assessment."

In theory, management has great flexibility in selecting techniques for testing key controls. It does not have to employ the same techniques (or even the same sampling criteria) as the external auditor. However:

> **KEY POINT:**
> TESTING KEY CONTROLS
>
> Management should always consider the total cost of its Section 404 program, which includes the external auditor's fees. Management can minimize its total costs by maximizing the degree to which the external auditor can reduce its hours through reliance on management testing.

- The testing techniques should clearly provide a reasonable individual sufficient assurance that the controls are operating effectively as documented.

- If self-assessment techniques are used (see below), there should be a reasonable level of independent confirmation of the self-assessment.

- Testing needs to provide assurance that the controls are operating effectively at year-end, as that is when the formal assessment is made. For tests performed earlier in the year, steps should be taken to update and roll forward the test results. Techniques that can be used include a limited re-performance of the earlier tests using fourth-quarter transactions, or obtaining re-certifications by process owners of their key controls.

- Testing needs to be performed by competent and trained individuals. A number of organizations are requiring operating management and staff to perform regular testing of their controls. While that may appear to be cost-effective (e.g., it may free internal audit specialists to focus on valuable operational, compliance, and other controls audits), management may need to provide objective reviews and retesting to ensure the tests are performed in accordance with quality standards and the results are reflective of actual operations. This additional review and testing might be performed by internal audit staff or a separate controls testing group. Management should consider the total costs of testing and the most efficient use of resources when staffing the testing program. See chapter 15 for a discussion of internal audit's role.

This document does not explore in depth the testing techniques that are available. Management should select the approach most suitable for the organization after consultation with experts, including the internal auditor. Some of the techniques include:

- Traditional testing of controls, such as:

  - Performance of walkthroughs, which confirm the adequacy of the documentation and the design of the controls to meet the control objectives.

  - Inquiry, examination, and inspection of related documents to confirm that the control appears to be performed consistently as documented.

  - Re-performance of a sample of transactions to confirm that the control is being performed effectively.

- Continuous auditing/monitoring of controls and/or transactions, which includes the testing of activity on a more continuous basis. This is generally assisted with software that selects the transactions to be reviewed (see chapter 11). The distinction between continuous auditing and monitoring is that auditing is performed by the internal audit or other independent assurance activity and monitoring is performed by management.

  There are essentially two forms:

  - Continuous auditing/monitoring of controls. For example, software can be used to monitor changes to automated controls in a SAP environment (configurable controls) and test to ensure they were approved in the system by the appropriate manager. This test provides assurance that the automated control continues to operate as intended (assuming its operation was tested earlier).

  - Continuous auditing/monitoring of transactions. An example would be a test that identifies purchase orders issued in excess of approved requisitions. The software would report exceptions for assessment as they occur.

In the first, the test confirms that the control is in place and operating as intended; any change was approved by the manager. The second is not a direct test of a control. It identifies exceptions that could indicate that a control is not operating as intended. These exceptions are then tested.

- Management self-assessment. There are several varieties of this technique, including *management's daily interaction with its controls* as discussed in the SEC guidance. Typically, management is asked to assess and confirm the operation of controls using a questionnaire or similar periodic survey. Management needs to consult with testing experts to ensure that the results of any self-assessment provide reasonable, objective evidence that the controls are operating as assessed. The risk is that the individuals performing the assessment may not have direct knowledge of the operation of the control or may not perform a rigorous assessment that verifies the consistency of the control's execution. (Management rarely has an incentive for reporting that it is not complying with policies or required procedures.)

  I have recommended that self-assessment be used to assess whether the COSO principles are achieved. Self-assessment can only be relied upon without testing of key controls where the risk is lower and the need for objective evidence is less.

The external auditors are required to do walkthroughs of key processes and controls, which help confirm the accuracy of the documentation and the adequacy of the design of the controls. Walkthroughs by management can, in some cases, be relied on by the external auditors and reduce total costs.[1] Walkthroughs by management are highly recommended, especially when there have been process or staff changes, as they will detect errors early and ensure management:

- Has a clear and current understanding of the processes and their operation.

- Can identify and correct potential issues early.

- Will perform more efficient testing, as documentation issues have been removed.

- Makes more efficient use of the external auditors' time by ensuring the currency, completeness, and accuracy of the documentation.

Earlier it was stated that management "has great flexibility in selecting techniques to use for testing its key controls." The "in theory" reservation was included because management should always consider the total cost of its Sarbanes-Oxley program. That total cost includes the external auditors' fees. Management can minimize its total costs by maximizing the degree to which the external auditors can reduce their hours through reliance on management testing.

It is still unclear to what extent the external auditors are able to reduce their hours through reliance on management testing when that testing is other than traditional. This is a developing area and merits continued monitoring. However, for the areas where the external auditors are required to perform independent testing and cannot rely on management testing (e.g., control areas assessed as high risk), management may be able to employ less traditional, more cost-effective methods.

A. TESTING AUTOMATED CONTROLS

In most cases, individuals with IT audit expertise will test the automated controls; however, management may request IT staff to perform the tests. This is acceptable but may not allow the external auditors to rely on management testing to reduce the scope of their work.

Where there are good change management controls within ITGC over an application, management may decide to test only a sample of automated controls each year. The principle, called "benchmarking," is described in the PCAOB Staff Questions and Answers "Auditing Internal Control over Financial Reporting" issued on May 16, 2005. The key sections in the quote below are italicized.

> "In general, to render an opinion as of the date of management's assessment, the auditor needs to test controls every year. This type of evidence is needed regardless of whether controls were found to be effective at the time of the prior annual assessments or whether those controls have changed since that time, because even if nothing significant changed about the company—the business model, employees, organizational structure, etc.—controls that were effective last year may not be effective this year due to error, complacency, distraction, and other human conditions that result in the inherent limitations in internal control over financial reporting. *Automated application controls, however, will continue to perform a given control (for example, aging of accounts receivable, extending prices on invoices, performing edit checks) in exactly the same manner until the program*

is changed. Entirely automated application controls, therefore, are generally not subject to breakdowns due to human failure and this feature allows the auditor to 'benchmark' or 'baseline' these controls.

"If general controls over program changes, access to programs, and computer operations are effective and continue to be tested, and if the auditor verifies that the automated application control has not changed since the auditor last tested the application control, the auditor may conclude that the automated application control continues to be effective without repeating the prior year's specific tests of the operation of the automated application control. The nature and extent of the evidence that the auditor should obtain to verify that the control has not changed may vary depending on the circumstances, including depending on the strength of the company's program change controls.

"When using a benchmarking strategy for a particular control, the auditor also should consider the importance of the effect of related files, tables, data, and parameters on the consistent and effective functioning of the automated application control. For example, an automated application for calculating interest income might be dependent on the continued integrity of a rate table used by the automated calculation.

"To determine whether to use a benchmarking strategy, the auditor should evaluate the following factors. As these factors increase in significance, the control being evaluated should be viewed as well suited for benchmarking. As these factors decrease in significance, the control being evaluated should be viewed as less suited for benchmarking. These factors are:

- The extent to which the application control can be matched to a defined program within an application;

- The extent to which the application is stable (i.e., there are few changes from period to period); and whether a report of the compilation dates of all programs placed in production is available and is reliable. (This information may be used as evidence that controls within the program have not changed.)

"Benchmarking automated application controls can be especially effective for companies using purchased software when the possibility of program changes is remote—for example, when the vendor does not allow access or modification to the source code.

"At some point, the benchmark of an automated application control should be reestablished. To determine whether to reestablish a benchmark, the auditor should evaluate the following factors:

- The effectiveness of the IT control environment, including controls over application and system software acquisition and maintenance, access controls and computer operations;

- The auditor's understanding of the effects of changes, if any, on the specific programs that contain the controls;

- The nature and timing of other related tests; and

- The consequences of errors."

The principle needs to be applied to each automated control in turn, examining whether: (a) the software has been changed since the last time it was tested, (b) whether there are sound change management processes and controls relative to the software, and (c) whether the control is of such significance that risk demands it be tested every year.

Before using benchmarking to help decide which automated controls require testing and the level of testing, it is important to meet with the external auditor. Even though the PCAOB has referenced benchmarking, each firm—and each partner within that firm—has different ideas on whether and to what extent it is acceptable. If management decides to reduce its testing of automated controls because of benchmarking, and the auditor does not accept benchmarking, the auditor will probably decide to perform its own expensive testing of the automated controls.

As will be discussed later in chapter 11, technology is now available that management can use to monitor changes to key automated controls, particularly *configurable controls*. An example of a configurable control is the three-way match in accounts payable where the company is using SAP systems; vendor invoices are matched against purchase orders and receiving documents before they are approved by the system for payment. The operation of the control is governed by its configuration or settings, which include whether the control is on or off; for which transactions it is on; whether invoices are matched against both orders and receipts or just orders; the tolerance level of mismatches; who receives notices of mismatches; and so forth. For the control to be operating as desired, all of these settings must be at the approved level. The auditor is concerned with changes to the configuration settings and technology is now available that will monitor and report such changes for review. If appropriate management is obtaining and acting on these reports, that may constitute effective change control and allow benchmarking to be applied.

In principle, when a company has invested in effective and consistent change management controls, it should have increased assurance that the software—including automated controls—will provide the required functionality consistently. Management should consider this when planning which automated controls to test. Even if no changes have been made, it is advisable to test at least a sample.

Another form of automated control is an *inherent* control. These are controls that are essentially hard-coded and never changed. A typical example is the automated control that ensures that journal entries balance (debits equal credits). Most external audit firms accept that these inherent controls do not change, there is no risk as a result, and therefore no need to test them. (See the PCAOB May 16, 2005, guidance quoted previously.)

Each of the automated controls, including key reports, needs to be tested unless benchmarking applies or they are inherent controls; an individual with IT audit experience will usually be able to identify the most appropriate test. Testing will normally consist of one or more of the following:

- Use of test data to confirm the proper operation of the control. The auditor, or IT staff with auditor review and approval, will enter transactions in the test environment and confirm the control operates as documented.

- Examination of related application code or settings—a common technique when SAP or Oracle Financials is the application and where configuration tables can be reviewed. The auditor must have a solid understanding of the software configurations or code to perform this test.

- Use of separate audit software to re-perform the functionality. For example, the auditor may use ACL or a BusinessObjects report to select and age open accounts receivable transactions and compare the results to the reports used by management.

- Manual re-performance of the control. In a few cases, where the control is not complex and the data not voluminous, the auditor may be able to recalculate totals or otherwise re-perform the specific functionality of the key control.

Unless there are concerns in ITGC that indicate a high risk of unauthorized or untested changes to automated controls, they need only be tested once each year (subject to benchmarking, as discussed previously). If IT general control issues indicate there is a significant risk that unauthorized, unapproved, or untested changes may be made to the automated controls, the frequency of testing should be increased with special attention given to year-end closing processes.

B. TESTING INDIRECT ENTITY-LEVEL CONTROLS

When it comes to obtaining assurance of the design and operation of indirect controls, such as the ethical values of the organization and the effectiveness of audit committee oversight, management again has more options than the external auditor. This is because, as recognized by the SEC and previously in AS 2, management has more direct exposure to and knowledge of its operations.

I have recommended that management provide a self-assessment for all of the 17 COSO principles and identify key indirect controls to test for high-risk areas. Management should review each key indirect control and determine the more appropriate method to obtain assurance. Methods include:

- Traditional sampling and testing (e.g., reviewing audit committee minutes to confirm the members reviewed the interim and annual financial statements).

- Surveys (e.g., surveying all or a substantial portion of the employees and obtaining their confidential assessment of the ethical environment, conformance to company policy, and so forth).

The external auditor may be able to rely on or join management in performing tests of indirect controls. Management should explore this possibility with the external auditor during annual planning.

Assessing the Adequacy of Controls, Including Assessing Deficiencies

If all key controls are properly identified, assessed as adequately designed, and the results of testing indicates they are all operating effectively, management will be able to assess its overall system of ICFR as effective. But, in reality, exceptions are identified in testing. A number of key controls could be deemed to be missing, deficient in design, or not operating effectively.

Management needs to decide whether these deficiencies mean that the system of internal control does not provide a reasonable level of assurance that there will not be material errors in future financial statements. This is achieved by assessing each control deficiency in turn to determine the likelihood of an error in the financial statements and its potential magnitude. Each deficiency is assessed to determine whether it is *material, significant,* or neither. Then, management needs to determine whether a combination of deficiencies[1] is likely to represent a risk (i.e., an *aggregated* risk) that is material or significant.

Although the scope of both management's and the external auditors' assessment of internal control is focused on the risk of a material misstatement of the financials, any deficiencies have to be assessed first to determine whether they are material

KEY POINTS:
ASSESSING THE ADEQUACY OF CONTROLS

- ► If all the key controls are properly identified, assessed as adequately designed, and the results of testing indicates they are all operating effectively, management is able to assess its overall system of internal control over financial reporting as effective.

- ► This evaluation requires an exercise of judgment, based on an assessment of what constitutes reasonable assurance under the circumstances, not on the mechanical application of a predetermined probability formula.

weaknesses, and then whether they are significant deficiencies. Only material weaknesses affect management's assessment and have to be disclosed in the annual financial statements; however, significant deficiencies must be identified and reviewed with the audit or equivalent committee.

Why worry about significant deficiencies if they do not have to be disclosed?

- If left untreated, the risk could increase and become a material weakness.

- If they are not addressed or, worse, repeated, this could be interpreted as a failure to give internal control sufficient attention—leading the external auditors to raise their risk level.

- Deficiencies in internal control very often represent a business risk beyond the risk to financial reporting. For example, a control deficiency might indicate a risk that reports used as a basis for decisions by management and the board contain errors.

The following definitions use the terms *material error,* as discussed above, and *reasonable possibility.* The latter is related to the term *reasonable assurance,* means that there is at least a reasonable likelihood, and is generally understood to be in the 5 percent to 10 percent probability range.

A *material weakness* is one where there is at least a *reasonable possibility* that an error that is *material* to the financial statements would neither be prevented nor detected within a reasonable period of time. It is defined the same way in the SEC and PCAOB guidance:

> "...a deficiency, or a combination of deficiencies, in internal control over financial reporting, such that there is a reasonable possibility that a material misstatement of the company's annual or interim financial statements will not be prevented or detected on a timely basis."

A *significant* deficiency is less severe. It was redefined in AS 5 and the SEC guidance for management:

> "...a deficiency, or a combination of deficiencies, in internal control over financial reporting that is less severe than a material weakness yet important enough to merit attention by those responsible for oversight of the company's financial reporting."

External audit firms historically adopted a 2004 framework for assessing deficiencies: *A Framework for Evaluating Control Exceptions and Deficiencies.*[2] However, the framework was never endorsed by the regulators. Management should understand the process followed by its external auditors (which is often an updated version of the framework). However, there is no requirement for management to follow precisely the same process.

Management should adopt a principles-based approach, relying on its judgment rather than a strict rules-based approach. The PCAOB similarly advised external auditors in a November 2005 report to rely on their professional judgment when assessing deficiencies:

> "This evaluation requires an exercise of judgment, based on an assessment of what constitutes reasonable assurance under the circumstances, not on the mechanical application of a predetermined probability formula. Inspectors observed, however, that the quest for quantitative rules of thumb in the application of the definitions described above may have resulted in some auditors exercising less judgment than the standard requires in this area. Many engagement teams used a framework developed through the collective effort of nine firms for evaluating deficiencies. That framework uses terms such as 'gross exposure,' 'adjusted exposure,' and 'upper-limit deviation rate.' The statistical precision suggested by these terms may have driven auditors' decision-making process unduly toward simplistic quantitative thresholds and away from the qualitative evaluation that may have been necessary in the circumstances.

> "This evaluation framework can result in decisions that are consistent with the provisions of Auditing Standard No. 2. Further, the use of the framework promoted consistency among different audit teams within and across firms. Nevertheless, the framework is not a substitute for the professional judgment that Auditing Standard No. 2 requires. Moreover, using this framework could, in some cases, lead auditors to spend more time evaluating the severity of a deficiency than otherwise would be necessary."

Management's process must ensure the following are considered:

1. **Has the true deficiency been identified?** Often, what appears to be a control deficiency is the symptom and not the root cause. For example, if account reconciliations are not being performed consistently on a timely basis, the root cause may be that

the individuals charged with that duty do not have sufficient time or information. Perhaps the control is not being performed with the necessary quality because of a failure to attract, retain, or train people with the necessary skills or experience.

A root cause analysis may identify a defect in one or more of the COSO principles, because the defect identified by the root cause analysis is not limited to the specific direct key control that failed but has more general implications.

In this case, both the failure of the direct key control and the weakness related to the principle in question should be identified as deficiencies and assessed.

2. Could there be an error in the financial statements as a result of the control deficiency (or combination of deficiencies)? If the answer is no, the process can stop and the deficiency assessed as neither significant nor material. Management should further reassess whether this should remain a key control.

With respect to deficiencies in IT general controls, management should follow the risk assessment in reverse order. They should identify what IT control objective is impacted by the deficiency and to what extent; whether the IT control objective should be considered not to have been achieved; what applications and critical IT functionality the IT control objective addresses; what critical IT functionality is involved; and what risk there is of an error in the financials.[3]

Indirect controls also require special handling to determine what controls and processes may be impacted. It is not sufficient to simply say these controls are pervasive. Instead, management needs to address specifics relative to risk to the financial statements. For example, if there are problems hiring trained accounting staff, what processes and controls are involved? In addition, are there sufficient management-level reviews and key controls that would detect or prevent errors? It would be unusual to conclude that an indirect entity-level control represented a material weakness, because its effect on the financial statements is indirect.

However, having said that it would be unusual, it certainly can and does happen. At one company, the Sarbanes-Oxley program leader informed the audit committee that none of the individuals involved in the financial close (including the preparation of the financial statements for filing, with necessary notes and other disclosures) had a relevant accounting certification. If this had been at year-end, it probably would have been identified as a material weakness because of the higher than acceptable risk of failing to comply with accounting standards.

When assessing deficiencies, it is important to consider why the control failed. In many cases, the *root cause* lies in the failure to satisfy one or more of the COSO principles, such as the competency, workload, or experience of the individuals involved in performing the control. Both a deficiency in the direct control and with respect to the COSO principle should be identified and assessed. As an example, the accounting service center in one company had control failures in one area during initial testing. During the next series of tests, those controls passed but another set failed. That pattern continued for a third set of tests, at which time the Sarbanes-Oxley leader informed management that the root cause lay in a failure of leadership, supervision, and the ability to retain trained staff. This was reported to the audit committee as a potential material weakness, as there was an unacceptable level of risk that key controls would fail (even if we didn't know which ones).

3. Are there compensating or mitigating controls (they must be identified as key controls, tested, and found to be effective before they can be relied on)? To what extent do they reduce the risk? If the answer is that the risk is fully addressed, the process can stop and the deficiency assessed as neither significant nor material. Management should further reassess whether this should remain a key control as it may be redundant.

4. Could the deficiency result in a material misstatement of the financials? The assessment must consider where the error would occur in the financial statements. It is relatively straightforward when the error is in the P&L. However, if the effect is only on balance sheet accounts, the error should be considered using a materiality gauge related to that account rather than the traditional P&L measure.

If the error would affect a disclosure, management needs to consider whether the error is material relative to the disclosed amounts and the significance to the investors, and potentially the regulators, of the specific disclosure. One measure that might be considered is whether the identification

> **KEY POINTS:**
> MATERIAL DEFICIENCIES
>
> ► Does management truly believe and would a reasonable person concur that the probability of a material error in future financial statements, which would not be detected by other controls, is in the 5 percent to 10 percent range or more?
>
> ► Would the deficiency prevent a prudent official from concluding that he or she has reasonable assurance that transactions are recorded as necessary to permit the preparation of financial statements in conformity with generally accepted accounting principles?

of an error of such an amount in a prior period's financial statements would result in needing to restate those financials; however, restatement due to a technicality that is not material to an investor decision should not be treated as a material weakness just because it led to a restatement.

5. **Is the risk of a material misstatement reasonably possible?** The next step is to assess the likelihood of that happening. As previously stated, *reasonably likely* is generally considered to be in the 5 percent to 10 percent range.

6. **Would a reasonable individual assess the deficiency as material?** This is the key *acid test*. Given that management may not assess its system of ICFR as effective once it identifies a material weakness, it should ask additional questions to validate the assessment of a deficiency as material.

   a. Does management truly believe and would a reasonable person concur that the probability of a material error in future financial statements, which would not be detected by other controls, is in the 5 percent to 10 percent range or more? In its November 30, 2005, report, the PCAOB stated:

   > "The definitions in the standard...are designed to lead to a determination as to whether the deficiency would prevent a prudent official from concluding that he or she has reasonable assurance that transactions are recorded as necessary to permit the preparation of financial statements in conformity with generally accepted accounting principles.

   > "Further, the terms 'probable,' 'reasonably possible,' and 'remote' should not be understood to provide for specific quantitative thresholds. Proper application of these terms involves a qualitative assessment of probability. Therefore, the evaluation of whether a control deficiency presents a 'more than remote' likelihood of misstatement can be made without quantifying the probability of occurrence as a specific percentage."

   b. If the assessment of a deficiency is based on prior period errors, perhaps resulting in the restatement of prior period financials, is it reasonable to assess the current condition of internal controls (and therefore identify a material weakness) as ineffective?

This issue (assessing controls following a restatement) has become topical. While some external auditors have taken the position that there must be a material weakness if the financials are being restated, that is neither the position of the SEC nor the PCAOB.

AS 5 describes the "restatement of previously issued financial statements to reflect the correction of a material misstatement" as an indicator of a material weakness, but has not directed that it must be assessed as such.

Both the SEC and PCAOB have indicated that while there is at least a significant deficiency, the underlying facts and circumstances must be considered. For example, if controls are improved in the current period by hiring additional technical accountants who then identify prior period accounting errors, then the current condition of internal controls is sound. This is because the material weakness was in the prior—and not in the current—period. On the other hand, if the error was detected by the external auditors and should have been, but was not, detected internally, this may indicate a material weakness in the internal staff's technical competence.

7. If the deficiency is not a material weakness, should it be disclosed to the audit committee as a significant deficiency? Significant deficiencies must be reported only to the audit or equivalent committee, and management is not required to disclose them in either the quarterly or annual reports filed with the SEC.

Management should give strong consideration to sharing any issues with the audit committee that are borderline significant deficiencies because this is prudent. It should also be noted that the remediation of a significant deficiency is probably[4] a material change in the system of internal control and should be reported in the interim period within which it occurs.

Material weaknesses must be considered and will affect both the quarterly Section 302 certification and the annual Sarbanes-Oxley assessment, if they are not corrected before year-end. Because the Sarbanes-Oxley assessment is as of year-end, management has the opportunity to achieve a clean opinion if it can identify the deficiency early, implement corrective actions, and test the corrected operations before year-end. The external auditors also should test the operation of remediated controls.

Chapter 10

MANAGEMENT'S REPORT ON INTERNAL CONTROLS: THE END PRODUCT

WHETHER IN THE annual assessment for Sarbanes-Oxley or the quarterly certification for Section 302, the language of management's report will be based substantially on specific regulatory requirements (especially in the case of Section 302) and the advice of counsel. However, there are certain drivers that management should consider:

1. Management has a great deal of latitude in describing the condition of its internal controls. The only formal requirement is that it not assess the controls as effective when there is a material weakness. Other requirements are being defined over time as the SEC responds to filings and sets expectations for content (counsel can advise on these matters).

2. The assessment should clearly describe management's opinion. What is the true condition of the system of internal control at the end of the year? Is it sufficiently robust to provide reasonable assurance that material errors will be either prevented or detected? The investor

> **KEY POINTS:**
> THE END PRODUCT
>
> ► Management has a great deal of latitude in describing the condition of its internal controls. The only formal requirement is that it not assess the controls as effective when there is a material weakness.
>
> ► The assessment should clearly describe management's opinion. What is the true condition of the system of internal control at the end of the year? Is it sufficiently robust to provide reasonable assurance that material errors will either be prevented or detected? The investor should be able to read the assessment and understand whether the company has adequate controls to run the business and report the results.

should be able to read the assessment and understand whether the company has adequate controls to provide reliable financial statements. (This is especially true when there is pressure to report a material weakness as a result of accounting errors in a prior period. Management should determine whether the current system of internal control is adequate, providing reasonable comfort related to the reliability of future financial statements, and not report deficiencies it does not believe relate to the current condition or future filings. In these circumstances, management may feel pressure to follow the rules at the expense of the principles. The assessment should reflect management's assessment of the controls and not mislead the investor regarding their effectiveness.)

3. The root cause of deficiencies should be understood. Control failures may be symptoms of a larger problem related to resources or management. The overall system will not be corrected until the larger problem is resolved, and, when known, the root cause should be reported. That is the true deficiency.

4. When deficiencies are reported, sufficient related information should be provided to enable the investor to understand their significance, the risk they represent, and how management will ensure the integrity of future financial statements.

Using Technology in the Sarbanes-Oxley Program

THERE IS NO question that technology can improve both the efficiency and the effectiveness of the Sarbanes-Oxley program in all but the smallest company. Consideration should be given to each of the following, which are discussed in more detail below:

- Sarbanes-Oxley program management, including automated working papers, action item follow-up, assessment of deficiencies, and status reporting

- Risk monitoring

- Testing tools

- Management self-assessments and employee surveys

Some software solutions will contain functionality in multiple areas. Each company should build the business case for software acquisition based on its specific needs.

It is important to recognize that there are multiple sources for this software. They include:

- Software acquired specifically for Sarbanes-Oxley

- Software acquired for multiple use within the company, including Sarbanes-Oxley

- Software that is already owned by the company. Very often, the software used to perform key controls can be used to test those controls.

A. Software to Manage the Overall Sarbanes-Oxley Program

In the early days of Sarbanes-Oxley, a number of vendors (including the accounting and consulting firms) offered software to help companies manage their Sarbanes-Oxley programs. Unfortunately, early Sarbanes-Oxley software often failed to deliver the necessary benefits and most organizations relied on Microsoft's Office solutions (i.e., Excel and Word). But, over the last few years, vendors have made significant enhancements and all organizations should at least consider today's solutions.[1]

Software will generally include the following capabilities:

- A repository where financial reporting risks can be identified and assessed. In some solutions, functionality is included to help identify significant accounts and locations. Ideally, the identification of significant accounts and locations can be repeated (preferably quarterly) to confirm they have not changed since the initial risk assessment.

- A repository where key controls (and non-key controls, if required) are documented. Preferably, these are linked both to the financial reporting risks and to the testing of the controls. The results of the latest testing should be shown, indicating whether the test has been performed; whether deficiencies were identified; and whether the deficiencies were assessed as material weakness, significant deficiencies, or insignificant.

- The ability to assign key controls for testing and maintain a test schedule.

- Automated working papers to record the results of testing.

- The assessment of deficiencies identified in testing, together with workflow and status reporting for related corrective actions.

- The ability to generate reports showing the status of the program.

The value that is provided is primarily in efficiency. Instead of managing multiple MS-Excel spreadsheets for risk assessment and the scheduling of work, and a volume of MS-Word documents to document the work performed, everything can be done in the single system. Status reports are available almost at the touch of a button and corrective action follow-up is automated. This value can be significant, far exceeding the cost of the software.

Some solutions also include a degree of automated testing of key controls. While these are generally more expensive, the value derived is also higher.

B. Risk Monitoring

An interesting use of technology is to alert the Sarbanes-Oxley program manager that the risk of a control failure has increased. Consider the following:

- Software is used to monitor trends in the volume and value of credit memos, with emphasis on the first month of each quarter. This is primarily a technique used to detect a revenue recognition fraud such as when arrangements are made with customers to send them inflated invoices, followed once the books have been closed for the quarter by credit memos. Revenue recognition fraud is clearly a risk to the financial statements.

- Reports from human resources indicate a surge in resignations in the corporate accounting function. Even if the positions are filled quickly by competent personnel, the risk of control failure in that department has increased.

- Sales in Australia exceed forecast by 200 percent. This was found by a financial auditor running BusinessObjects or Cognos queries against the corporate data warehouse, and this event might bring related accounts and processes into scope for the Sarbanes-Oxley program.

- An adverse trend in product returns is evident in reports from the financial analyst group. There is now a higher risk related to related revenue, unless management increases reserves.

- Using information in the change management system, the IT audit team identifies that the volume of application software changes has increased significantly. The reasons for the increase should be investigated as they might be the result of "fixes" to correct software bugs, or other failure of IT general controls processes.

Note that in some of these examples, the Sarbanes-Oxley team did not use independent software. They used existing reports (from human resources and financial analysts) or ran their own analyses using the process owner's systems (e.g., the application change management system).

This kind of monitoring can help identify potential problems early. It is recommended, especially where existing reports or software—or software acquired to assist in testing—can be used.

C. TESTING TOOLS

Software can assist in a number of ways, but it is unlikely that a single tool will help with the testing of all key controls—manual and automated, business process and IT general controls, direct and indirect entity-level controls.

Examples of uses of technology in testing include:

- Sampling transactions for testing. This might be done using statistical sampling or other rule (e.g., every manual journal entry between defined dates with entries in excess of a certain value that are posted into significant accounts at significant locations).

- Testing the population of transactions against defined rules to identify potential control failures. These transactions might be within business processes (e.g., accounts payable) or IT general controls (e.g., application change control). For example, software might be used to compare vendor invoices against purchase orders to validate that they match within the approved tolerance level. Another example is using software to monitor application code changes and confirm that they were approved by the appropriate IT and user managers.

- Confirming that automated controls, specifically *configurable* controls in Oracle or SAP ERP systems, have either not been changed or the changes were approved. Techniques include monitoring a log of changes to the automated control configurations: if there were no documented changes, the test confirms this; if there were changes, the software can either route the changes for manual verification of approvals, or may be able to examine the transaction records to see who approved the change and confirm it was the appropriate individual.

- Software is especially valuable in testing access to enterprise business applications, and sometimes applications used in IT general controls processes. Ideally, the software used by the company to manage systems access also has the ability to provide reports that can be used by the auditor. Otherwise, the auditor might work with IT to find other ways to obtain reports, for example, showing:

  - Combinations of access that represent a risk to key controls (i.e., segregation of duties issues).

  - Who has access to specific functions that must be controlled as part of a key control (e.g., approval of journal entries, or super-user capabilities).

  - What individuals with apparent "excessive" access (such as people with the ability both to approve a new vendor and approve payment to that vendor) have done with that access, if anything.

- Re-performing controls, such as the calculation of reserves or allowances. In some complex situations, such as the calculation of a warranty reserve, the auditor might want to develop software to approximate the company's calculation. Due to the complexity of the calculation, this might not be able to provide precise confirmation of the calculation, but it might be able to provide assurance that it is not materially incorrect.

D. Management Self-Assessments and Employee Surveys

These two techniques are especially useful for *indirect entity-level controls.* Software for each can improve the efficiency of the testing process.

Management self-assessments and surveys can be done using standalone software. But, ideally the software used to manage the Sarbanes-Oxley program and schedule the testing also has these capabilities. The Sarbanes-Oxley program manager is able to select a control or combination of controls for self-assessment or use in a survey, choose one of those techniques as the testing method, and route the appropriate questionnaire (or similar) to the appropriate managers and staff for completion. The software will track completion, perform follow-up requests, and summarize the results.

Chapter 12

ASSESSING THE EFFICIENCY OF THE SARBANES-OXLEY PROGRAM

MOST WILL AGREE that the Sarbanes-Oxley requirement has improved the quality of internal control systems through increased attention by both management and the external auditor. However, there is less than universal agreement that the improvement has been justified relative to the enormous cost.

The following checklist may help management teams complete a self-assessment and ensure their Sarbanes-Oxley program is efficient.

1. Has operating management taken ownership of its processes and documentation, rather than leaving it to the Sarbanes-Oxley team or the internal audit activity?

2. Does operating management update all process and control documentation promptly throughout the year and not just when testing starts? Is there an effective change management process in place, including the timely assessment of process changes for their potential impact on key controls?

> **KEY POINT:**
> EFFICIENCY
>
> Is the Sarbanes-Oxley program assessed for effectiveness on a continuing basis, to ensure it is improved as the organization learns from experience and benefits from changes in regulations or their interpretation?

3. Is operating management committed to assess and remediate all control deficiencies promptly? Is the root cause of each deficiency being addressed? If not, the control failure is likely to be repeated. In situations where remediation is not justified based on management's assessment of risk and cost, is management committed to communicating that decision

promptly so the effect on its overall assessment of controls can be identified and discussed with senior management?

4. Has a top-down, risk-based approach been used to identify the key controls? Is management confident that all identified key controls are truly key? Has the design of the related processes been reviewed to determine whether changes can result in fewer and more effective controls, relying more on automated controls or on higher-level controls (e.g., detailed reconciliations and flux analyses)? The fewer the controls to test, the lower the cost.

5. Is management of the Sarbanes-Oxley program at a sufficiently high level within the organization to:

   - Influence operating management relative to completion of its responsibilities?

   - Communicate effectively with executive management the program's progress and potential issues?

   - Negotiate as needed with the external auditor (e.g., to increase reliance on management testing, agree on key controls early, and address concerns as they arise)?

6. Is the use of internal resources optimized, including the use of internal auditors to perform testing or to validate testing performed by management staff?

7. Has overall staffing been optimized, reducing reliance on more expensive external consultants and testers?

8. Has reliance by the external auditor on management testing been optimized?

9. Does the external auditor follow a top-down, risk-based approach as required by AS 5?

10. Is there a detailed project plan:

    a. That includes a walk-through of all significant processes early in the year, preferably in the first quarter?

    b. With testing scheduled in such a way that all key controls are tested by midyear, with additional testing to update the results scheduled closer to year-end? This enables the external auditors to start their walkthroughs and testing early, providing time for management to address and remediate any deficiencies identified in either management or external auditor testing.

c. That includes all key activities required to complete the program, such as fraud risk assessment, consideration of any end-user computing issues, assessment of SSAE 16 reports from service providers, and so forth?

d. Detailing all required resources, including specialists (e.g., for IT or tax processes and controls), so they can be scheduled early?

e. With regular reporting to senior management that focuses on key metrics and issues, such as:

- Progress against timetables, highlighting steps that are or may be behind schedule?

- Percentage of key controls tested compared to their scheduled completion level?

- Number and percentage of key controls that are failing?

- Number of failed controls that are potentially significant to the Sarbanes-Oxley assessment?

- The number of failed controls where remediation will not be completed within 30 days, so senior management can focus on a timely completion?

- The number of key controls where remediation and retesting may not be completed with sufficient time for the external auditors to retest (these are likely to be open deficiencies at year-end)?

- Costs to date and projected through the end of the year?

- Potential resource issues?

- Other issues, such as coordination and concerns raised by the external auditors?

11. Has there been communication and coordination with all service providers to ensure that an SSAE 16 report will be available at the

appropriate time, and that early warning is provided of potential deficiencies being identified during the related attest work?

12. Finally, is the Sarbanes-Oxley program itself assessed for effectiveness on a continuing basis to ensure it is improved as the organization learns from experience and benefits from changes in regulations or their interpretation?

Chapter 13

An Efficient System of Internal Control Over Financial Reporting

When faced with the Sarbanes-Oxley requirements for internal control over financial reporting, many companies reacted by adding controls to their existing processes. These controls may have been based on a checklist of desired controls from a third party or other source of preferred controls.

What these companies did not do is review the design of their business processes and adapt them so that they both had the controls necessary to manage financial reporting risk and remained an efficient way to run the business. Instead, new controls were layered on top of existing business processes, making them less than efficient.

Most companies are now relatively comfortable that they understand the financial reporting risks in their business. This allows reflection on whether the related business processes and controls can be upgraded and made more efficient and effective. Consideration should be given to:

- Eliminating unnecessary controls. Many new controls were added in the early stages of Sarbanes-Oxley that are no longer considered key. These should be reviewed to determine whether they fill any important business need, and if not, be eliminated. Only about half of the companies responding to the Ernst & Young study mentioned earlier have rationalized their key controls in the last year.

- Identifying and addressing duplicative or redundant controls. When controls were added for Sarbanes-Oxley, they may have duplicated existing controls. For example, the prior process might have included a review by a supervisor of a transaction at the time it is recorded, but this was not considered sufficient for Sarbanes-Oxley and a manager review based on a monthly report added. It might be possible to streamline the process by combining the two controls or eliminating one. I have also seen situations where an automated control was added, but the existing manual control continued; this may happen because the department performing the manual control was not informed that the manual control was no longer required.

- Replacing multiple local controls with entity-level controls. This may involve delaying the detection of errors, so the risk to the business should be considered. According to the Ernst & Young study, 94 percent of companies have "fewer than a quarter of their key controls as entity-level controls." While there is no "ideal" number of entity-level controls, this may be an area of opportunity for many.

- Deploying technology to either replace manual with automated controls, or to support the implementation of entity-level controls based on reports of activity.

- Stepping back and reexamining the business processes—especially with the inevitable changes in the business since the processes were implemented—and the potential of new technology.

- Combining activities into a shared service center. While many companies have taken this action for some processes, they may not have performed a complete assessment and redesign of the entire process, and there may also be an opportunity to move additional processes into a shared service center.

While there are metrics that can be acquired from some third parties,[1] any redesign should take into account the need to address financial reporting risks. In addition, any measurement of the cost of the process should include the cost to test it for Sarbanes-Oxley purposes.

Chapter 14

Working With the External Auditor

WHILE IT IS not in theory necessary to work in a collaborative fashion with the external auditor, there are strong reasons to do so:

1. It is highly inefficient for management and the auditor to identify different financial reporting risks, materiality levels, significant accounts or locations, or key controls and—as a result—test different controls. The earlier the above are agreed, the lower the risk that management will have to change its scope and find that it failed to test locations (for example) that should have been included in scope, or performed tests of controls that did not need to be in scope.

2. Efficiencies are gained when the external auditor is able to rely on management's work. It is possible for the auditor to rely on management testing for as much as 80 percent or more for the testing of some key controls, resulting in significant fee reductions and reduced disruption to the business through their support of the testing. But the auditor must include this in the plan, and obtain comfort on both management's approach to testing and the adequacy of the testing program. It is inefficient for the auditor to assess and conclude on management's testing team and process after work has been completed, especially if that work is not up to the required standard and will have to be redone before reliance can be placed on it.

AS 5 contains this guidance for the external auditor:

"16. The auditor should evaluate the extent to which he or she will use the work of others to reduce the work the auditor might otherwise perform himself or herself. AU sec. 322, *The Auditor's Consideration of the Internal Audit*

Function in an Audit of Financial Statements, applies in an integrated audit of the financial statements and internal control over financial reporting.

"17. For purposes of the audit of internal control, however, the auditor may use the work performed by, or receive direct assistance from, internal auditors, company personnel (in addition to internal auditors), and third parties working under the direction of management or the audit committee that provides evidence about the effectiveness of internal control over financial reporting. In an integrated audit of internal control over financial reporting and the financial statements, the auditor also may use this work to obtain evidence supporting the auditor's assessment of control risk for purposes of the audit of the financial statements.

"18. The auditor should assess the competence and objectivity of the persons whose work the auditor plans to use to determine the extent to which the auditor may use their work. The higher the degree of competence and objectivity, the greater use the auditor may make of the work. The auditor should apply paragraphs .09 through .11 of AU sec. 322 to assess the competence and objectivity of internal auditors. The auditor should apply the principles underlying those paragraphs to assess the competence and objectivity of persons other than internal auditors whose work the auditor plans to use.

"Note: For purposes of using the work of others, competence means the attainment and maintenance of a level of understanding and knowledge that enables that person to perform ably the tasks assigned to them, and objectivity means the ability to perform those tasks impartially and with intellectual honesty. To assess competence, the auditor should evaluate factors about the person's qualifications and ability to perform the work the auditor plans to use. To assess objectivity, the auditor should evaluate whether factors are present that either inhibit or promote a person's ability to perform with the necessary degree of objectivity the work the auditor plans to use.

"Note: The auditor should not use the work of persons who have a low degree of objectivity, regardless of their level of competence. Likewise, the auditor should not use the work of persons who have a low level of competence regardless of their degree of objectivity. Personnel whose core function is to serve as a testing or compliance authority at the company, such as internal auditors, normally are expected to have greater competence and objectivity in performing the type of work that will be useful to the auditor.

"19. The extent to which the auditor may use the work of others in an audit of internal control also depends on the risk associated with the control being tested. As the risk associated with a control increases, the need for the auditor to perform his or her own work on the control increases."

While there continues to be a debate among internal auditors as to whether they should perform testing of key controls on behalf of management (see chapter 15), AS 5 makes it clear that the external auditors are more likely to rely on internal audit testing than testing by operating management. This is something, again, that should be decided as early in the planning process as possible.

3. One interesting opportunity is for the Sarbanes-Oxley team and the external auditor to coordinate walkthroughs, visits to overseas locations, and so forth. This can lead to a common understanding of those processes and the key controls, and minimizing disruption to those locations as they only have to accommodate one visit.

4. The level of trust that is obtained when the Sarbanes-Oxley team works well with the external auditor has great value. For example:

    a. The auditor is more likely to inform the Sarbanes-Oxley team promptly when questions or issues arise. When the Sarbanes-Oxley team is involved, working with management to understand issues surfaced from testing by the external auditor, those issues are much more likely to be addressed promptly and satisfactorily. The Sarbanes-Oxley team can be of great value to management if it is involved in these situations, so it can explain the concerns and answers to both parties (management and auditor).

> **KEY POINT:**
> WORKING WITH THE
> EXTERNAL AUDITOR
>
> "The level of trust that is obtained when the Sarbanes-Oxley team works well with the external auditor has great value."

    b. It is easier to obtain agreement on the significance of deficiencies and the required corrective action.

    c. The Sarbanes-Oxley manager is more likely to obtain information on the status of the external auditor's work when reports to management or the audit committee are required.

5. Another area of efficiency from collaboration is that when there are good relations and communication, there are channels to keep the external auditor current on changes that might affect their work—such as changes in the business or new computer systems. The external auditor is also informed when management finds problems, so they can delay their own testing until the issues are resolved. Surprising the auditor is never a good idea!

6. Management often feels that the external auditor does more work than necessary: includes more accounts and locations in scope; sets the materiality level too low; tests too many key controls; and does too much testing of those key controls. Management is far more likely to be able to influence the external auditor's work if relationships and communications are first class and there is mutual trust and respect—both of which have to be earned.

These are techniques that I have been able to use successfully to (a) improve relationships with the external auditor and (b) realize significant cost savings and efficiencies through increased reliance on management's work:

- Building personal relationships with the key members of the external audit team. In particular, the leader of the Sarbanes-Oxley program should establish open relationships with the audit firm partners responsible for the various key areas (including IT and tax).

- Setting the expectation that management and the auditor should work together for the benefit of both the company and the auditor.

- Persuading the CFO and the audit committee to reinforce the message that coordination and cooperation were expected. This is very important.

- Understanding what was important to the external auditor and endeavoring to build that into the Sarbanes-Oxley program.

- Sharing what was important to the Sarbanes-Oxley team and the company.

- Because the scoping would be based on this guide and the GAIT Methodology, providing the external audit partner with copies of both and meeting to determine whether they agreed or disagreed with the approaches they describe.

- Informing the external auditor as soon as practical of matters relevant to their work.

- Building an environment demonstrating mutual trust.

THE ROLE OF INTERNAL AUDIT

THERE IS A sharp divide among internal audit professionals as to whether the internal audit activity should play a significant role in the Sarbanes-Oxley program. In the first few years of Sarbanes-Oxley, management more often than not looked to internal audit as internal control experts to lead the development and implementation of the Sarbanes-Oxley program.

For example, a KPMG study in 2005 showed that internal audit:

- Was responsible for oversight of the Sarbanes-Oxley program at 15 percent of companies.

- Provided day-to-day project management at 31 percent of companies (it should be noted that several surveys on this topic produced very different results. A PricewaterhouseCoopers (PwC) study[1] in the same year reported that 56 percent of companies relied on internal audit for day-to-day project management).

- Was involved in documentation and testing of key controls at 85 percent of companies.

However, those internal audit activities were generally not given the resources necessary to perform the Sarbanes-Oxley work *in addition* to what they needed to meet their traditional and broader assurance responsibilities. As a result, internal audit groups became consumed by a narrow focus on Sarbanes-Oxley and cut back on audits of other risk areas. The PwC study referenced above reported that for 70 percent of companies in the first year of their Sarbanes-Oxley program, internal audit dedicated at least 50 percent of its resources to supporting the Sarbanes-Oxley program.

This caused concern among internal audit professionals, audit committees, the auditing firms, and a number of governance experts. They urged companies and their internal auditors to return to a more operational and traditional focus on risks and controls that extended beyond financial reporting. For example, Deloitte[2] commented:

"The dramatic increase in the workload of internal audit attributable to Sarbanes-Oxley wasn't always accompanied by an equal rise in resources, leading to a predictable outcome: The traditional work of the function—operational, systems, fraud investigations, and special project audit work—often took a back seat to the more pressing needs of regulatory compliance.

"For many internal audit departments, this shift toward Sarbanes-Oxley-related duties demands rebalancing. Meeting the requirements of the law is, obviously, important, but not to the detriment of other responsibilities. The function's all-encompassing focus on Sarbanes-Oxley, adopted out of necessity in the early years, should diminish going forward, and in its stead should be a more rational and considered distribution of duties."

PwC[3] had even stronger language:

"Internal audit organizations have been so consumed by Sarbanes-Oxley [sic] that other priorities are falling by the wayside. Simply put, the legislation is diverting internal audit resources from risk-based auditing, creating the potential for dire consequences. That's because a failure to address key strategic, operational, and compliance risk areas in an internal audit program undermines the effectiveness of internal audit, diminishes its strategic value to key stakeholders, and exposes the enterprise to greater operational and financial risks in the future."

Today, the number of internal audit activities involved in these three areas is lower (although KPMG and other firms have not updated their surveys, less formal studies show about half of companies are still using internal audit to perform Sarbanes-Oxley testing) and efficiencies have brought the level of effort down as well. Certainly, larger firms are more likely to have established internal control activities (or similar) within the corporate finance function that are responsible for the Sarbanes-Oxley program. But the concern remains among a number of internal audit leaders.

While there is a risk, as expressed above by Deloitte and PwC, there are also significant benefits when internal audit makes a contribution to the Sarbanes-Oxley program. These include:

- Internal audit practitioners are experts in internal control and their experience and insights contribute to an efficient and effective Sarbanes-Oxley program.

- When internal audit performs testing on behalf of management, it is more likely to be relied on by the external auditors, and this can result in significant savings on audit fees.

- Internal audit can perform combined or integrated audits that include both Sarbanes-Oxley testing and non-Sarbanes-Oxley work. The total number of audits performed, each of which management must support, is reduced.

- When internal audit tests Sarbanes-Oxley key controls, they are more likely to be able to recommend process and control enhancements than if the testing is performed by management.

- Internal audit is charged with providing assurance and consulting services on all major risks, including the risk of poor controls over financial reporting. They might be obliged to review and assess management's testing if they don't do it themselves, at greater cost to the company as a whole than if they did the testing.

Each company should weigh the risks and benefits of internal audit involvement in Sarbanes-Oxley. These considerations should be given significant attention by management and the board:

1. It is critical that internal audit have the resources to meet its commitments as documented in the charter. Its ability to provide assurance and consulting services on the organization's governance, risk management, and related control processes must not be impaired to the point that it cannot address issues of significance.

2. Internal audit may not perform a management function. It must remain independent and objective, consistent with The IIA's *International Standards for the Professional Practice of Internal Auditing*. It can, as a consulting service, facilitate the Sarbanes-Oxley program and provide day-to-day project management. It can also perform testing of key controls. However, the following are management functions that cannot be assigned to internal audit:

a. Responsibility for the Sarbanes-Oxley assessment and program. These typically rest with the CEO and CFO.

b. Making decisions relative to the Sarbanes-Oxley scope and program design. Internal audit may make recommendations, but management should make the final decision in each case.

c. Assessing whether a deficiency will be considered, for the purposes of management's assessment of ICFR, a material weakness. Internal audit should share its opinion, but the decision rests with management.

d. Assessing the overall adequacy of ICFR.

3. The decision should be based on what is best for the company as a whole, considering cost, risk, value, and the need to points in (2) above. While most CFOs and corporate controllers are interested in assigning the work to internal audit, and internal audit professionals would prefer the work to be handled by finance staff, both must put the interests of the company first.

Reference should also be made to guidance from The IIA in *Internal Auditing's Role in Sections 302 and 404 of the Sarbanes-Oxley Act,* which was released on May 26, 2004. Key points addressed in the document related to assistance with testing include:

"It is management's responsibility to ensure the organization is in compliance with the requirements of Sections 302 and 404 and other requirements of the Act, and this responsibility cannot be delegated or abdicated. Support for management in the discharge of these responsibilities is a legitimate role for internal auditors. The internal auditors' role in their organization's Sarbanes-Oxley project can be significant but also must be compatible with the overall mission and charter of the internal audit function. Regardless of the level and type of involvement selected, it should not impair the objectivity and capabilities of the internal audit function for covering the major risk areas of their organization. Internal auditors are frequently pressured to be extensively involved in the full compendium of Sarbanes-Oxley project efforts as the work is within the natural domain of expertise of internal auditing." (Executive Summary)

"Activities that are included in the internal auditor's recommended role in supporting the organization in meeting the requirements of Sections 302 and 404 include:

- Project Oversight.
- Consulting and Project Support.
- Ongoing Monitoring and Testing.
- Project Audit."

"Ongoing Monitoring and Testing

- Advise management regarding the design, scope, and frequency of tests to be performed.
- Independent assessor of management testing and assessment processes.
- Perform tests of management's basis for assertions.
- Perform effectiveness testing (for highest reliance by external auditors).
- Aid in identifying control gaps and review management plans for correcting control gaps.
- Perform follow-up reviews to ascertain whether control gaps have been adequately addressed.
- Act as coordinator between management and the external auditor as to discussions of scope and testing plans.
- Participate in disclosure committee to ensure that results of ongoing internal audit activities and other examination activities, such as external regulatory examinations, are brought to the committee for disclosure consideration."

The Relationship Between Governance, Risk Management, and Compliance; ERM; and Sarbanes-Oxley

OVER THE LAST few years, questions have been asked about governance, risk management, and compliance (GRC); enterprise risk management (ERM); and Sarbanes-Oxley:

- What is GRC and how does it relate to Sarbanes-Oxley? Should I have a "GRC program" that includes Sarbanes-Oxley compliance?

- Is GRC the same as ERM? What is the relationship?

- How do I efficiently integrate my Sarbanes-Oxley program with the enterprise-wide risk management program?

A. GRC and Sarbanes-Oxley

In its earliest incarnations, GRC was used most often to refer to the need to address the growth and complexity of laws and regulations impacting organizations, especially global companies. The cost of compliance was increasing at an alarming pace, especially with passage of the Sarbanes-Oxley Act, yet the risk of noncompliance remained relatively high. Issues related not only to the compliance and risk management programs but also to certain aspects of governance, such as oversight of these programs; the management of related standards, policies, and procedures; and the compliance activities of internal audit and other assurance groups.

While there is no consistent definition of the term, with analysts, vendors, and consultants tending to describe it somewhat differently, the best description comes from the independent, not-for-profit Open Compliance & Ethics Group (OCEG). Their *Red*

Book 2.0[1] includes a description of GRC that is business-oriented and focuses on driving performance, while considering and managing risk and staying in compliance.

The OCEG *Red Book* introduces GRC this way:

> "A number of key business processes help organizations achieve Principled Performance,[2] and processes under the areas of governance, risk management, and compliance are particularly critical to its success. Because there is significant overlap in the activities that underlie and support those broad areas, addressing them and all others that contribute to Principled Performance in an integrated fashion allows a consistent view of information and efficient application of resources that greatly enhance the power each individual process brings to the organization. We call that integrated approach 'GRC.'"

The more formal OCEG definition of GRC is:

> "A system of people, processes, and technology that enables an organization to:
>
> - Understand and prioritize stakeholder expectations.
> - Set business objectives that are congruent with values and risks.
> - Achieve objectives while optimizing risk profile and protecting value.
> - Operate within legal, contractual, internal, social, and ethical boundaries.
> - Provide relevant, reliable, and timely information to appropriate stakeholders.
> - Enable the measurement of the performance and effectiveness of the system."

This is an excellent definition that highlights risk management as an enabler of performance, and that the delivery of corporate results must be tempered by the need to remain in compliance.

Sarbanes-Oxley compliance is clearly one of the aspects of compliance that is included in GRC. The value that the GRC perspective brings to Sarbanes-Oxley compliance is the recognition that the Sarbanes-Oxley program might overlap or duplicate other compliance and assurance programs. For example:

- Key controls may include IT security practices that are also critical for compliance with data privacy regulations.

- Key controls may include approval procedures for payments to overseas agents, which are very important for compliance with the U.S. Foreign Corrupt Practices Act and the UK Bribery Act.

- Even if the key controls are different, the same areas and processes may be audited/tested by different groups. For example, controls over inventory might be tested both for Sarbanes-Oxley and International Organization for Standardization (ISO) purposes.

B. Implications for the Sarbanes-Oxley Program

Sarbanes-Oxley is only one of potentially many compliance obligations an organization might have to assess and test its controls. The GRC perspective highlights the possibility that if the Sarbanes-Oxley and other assessments (e.g., for privacy compliance purposes) are performed in silos and without any coordination, work might be duplicated. The result is not only extra cost but also more disruption of the business to support the assessment work.

The Sarbanes-Oxley team should, if at all possible, understand how its work might overlap with that of other assurance providers. Efficiencies may be obtained by coordination of efforts, such as the use of a joint team and joint audit, or reliance on the work of another assurance provider. The latter will typically require that the Sarbanes-Oxley team perform similar procedures to those the external auditors use to determine whether they can rely on management testing (see chapter 14).

I led a team at a prior employer that visited a plant in Malaysia. Members included:

- Internal auditors testing controls in a number of areas, including controls over financial reporting.

- External auditors who joined internal auditors for meetings to obtain an understanding of controls and coordinated with them to test controls and assess any deficiencies. They divided the controls to be tested with internal audit and shared working papers after testing had been completed.

- ISO quality auditors assessing compliance with ISO standards around inventory management and product quality.

- IT security personnel confirming compliance with corporate standards.

- Representatives of the Lean Manufacturing team, similarly confirming compliance with corporate standards.

As part of planning for the visit, the team agreed that they needed to reduce duplication of effort and only test each process and its controls once. They divided up the different areas of the business, shared audit objectives and programs, and planned the work so that all objectives were achieved and disruption to business operations was minimized. The results of the testing, including copies of the working papers, were shared.

Other companies have worked in a similar fashion to avoid redundant work. For example, if it is known that the corporate security team is going to audit a factory in France, and key controls for Sarbanes-Oxley include limiting access to physical inventory, the Sarbanes-Oxley manager can assess the adequacy of the corporate security department's procedures and planned testing of those key controls. If sufficient, the Sarbanes-Oxley team may be able rely on the corporate security team's testing. If not, the Sarbanes-Oxley manager may be able to persuade the corporate security team to make the necessary changes so that reliance is possible.

C. GRC AND ERM

Quite simply, the risk management referred to in GRC (the "R") is enterprisewide risk management (ERM). While some talk about the R in GRC referring to some subset, typically risks relating to compliance, that is not consistent with the definition of GRC recognized by the author—the OCEG definition referenced above.

D. SARBANES-OXLEY AND ERM

The Sarbanes-Oxley program is about managing the risk of material misstatement of the financials filed with the SEC, and ERM is about managing all risks to the organization. So it is logical that there is a relationship between the two.

The Sarbanes-Oxley program assesses and manages risk at a very detailed level, whereas ERM usually operates at a higher level. One way the two can work together effectively is as follows:

- The identification of specific financial reporting risks, the risk of control failures, and other risks managed by the Sarbanes-Oxley program is documented only in that program.

- The assessment of key controls is documented in the Sarbanes-Oxley program.

- The status and management of corrective actions, which must be tied back to individual key controls, is also handled in Sarbanes-Oxley.

- The *overall* assessment of whether financial reporting risks are adequate is recorded in the ERM program. Judgment is used (using the assessment of risks and controls in Sarbanes-Oxley) as to the overall level of risk of material misstatement.

- Monitoring of risks within ERM might identify changes with the potential of affecting the Sarbanes-Oxley program. For example, if the organization has decided to implement a new inventory management system, a number of risks might be identified and recorded in the ERM system (such as the risk of project cost overruns). The Sarbanes-Oxley team might be able to use the risk monitoring in ERM to identify potential changes that could impact the Sarbanes-Oxley program.

Continuous Improvement

ONCE THE SARBANES-OXLEY program is running well and seen to be efficient, it is tempting to move it to the back burner. Improvements and upgrades are no longer seen as a high priority.

However, the program is important. It must be effective (the risk associated with a material weakness is generally not tolerable) and even the cost of an efficient program is not insignificant.

The program should be reviewed regularly, preferably annually after the assessment has been completed. For example, an annual assessment might include:

- Completion of the checklist in chapter 12.

- A review of the year just completed to determine what could have been done better. This should include discussions with management and the external auditor to determine satisfaction levels and opportunities for improvement. Special attention should be given to the timing of planning, walkthroughs, and testing.

- An assessment of the technology that was employed, together with advances in technology, to determine whether changes should be made.

- What will change in the next year: systems, processes, organization, acquisitions or divestitures, and so forth? How will that affect the program?

To close, two quotes are meaningful:

"The arrogance of success is to think that what we did yesterday is good enough for tomorrow."

— *William Pollard*

"To think creatively, we must be able to look afresh at what we normally take for granted."

— *George Keller*

Chapter 18

The Impact of New Technology

THE *AUSTRALIAN* newspaper has described 2011 as "the most radical period of change in the history of digital technology. It has been the year cloud computing came of age, smash-hit consumer devices such as Apple's iPad invaded the corporate computing arena, and the market for mobile apps exploded."

As this technology is adopted within an organization, it will change business processes and key controls. For example:

- An individual will select items for purchase from a catalog, using his Apple iPad or iPhone. The "shopping cart" will be sent to his manager for approval on her mobile device. The business process now involves not only the enterprise purchasing application but functionality on mobile devices. The key control of approving the purchase has moved to a mobile device, and controls may be necessary to assure the identity of the approving manager.

- Significant applications will reside in the cloud. They may be in a private cloud (owned and operated by the company) or in a public company (operated by a service provider).

While it is difficult to predict the future, I believe that while the new technology will change business and IT processes, and the nature and location of key controls, the basic principles in this guide will remain appropriate. Understand the risks to financial reporting. Identify the combination of key controls necessary to test those controls. Test the controls and evaluate the overall system of internal control over financial reporting.

The future will be exciting—not only in how our personal and business lives will be changed by technology but how we will find ways to use technology to make our Sarbanes-Oxley programs even more efficient and effective.

NOTES

About the Third Edition

1. The first edition was published in 2006. The second edition was released in 2008.

How to Use This Guide

1. Although "Sarbanes-Oxley" is used to refer to the Sarbanes-Oxley Act, the term "Sarbanes-Oxley program" and similar terms refer to the assessment required under Section 404 of the Act.

Introduction

1. Many internal auditors have professional certifications in auditing, including The IIA's Certified Internal Auditor (CIA), which indicates they have demonstrated their understanding of internal controls and related auditing.

2. Included in the quarterly financial statements filed on Form 10-Q with the SEC.

Summary for the CEO and CFO

1. The guidance published by the SEC and PCAOB does not address this issue directly. However, there are indications in comments by officials with these organizations that the value of the Sarbanes-Oxley assessment is that it provides a level of comfort with respect to the reliability of future financial statements, assuming there is no significant change in the quality of the system of internal control. The quality of the system of internal control at the end of the reporting year is an indication of whether it is sufficiently robust to either prevent or detect material misstatements in financial statements that will be prepared under the processes and related controls that management has assessed. In addition, an assessment of the likelihood of any event is difficult, if not impossible, without

defining the period during which the event may occur. In this guide, I have taken the reasonable position that management's assessment should reflect the likelihood of a material misstatement in one or more of the next 12 months' financial statement filings.

Neither the SEC nor the PCAOB have publicly commented on this matter, and my position relative to 12 months—which would include the next annual financials on Form 10-K and interim reports on Form 10-Q—is a suggestion based on what I believe is reasonable.

2. Of note is this excerpt from Institutional Shareholder Services, *ISS U.S. Corporate Governance Policy - 2006 Updates*:

> "Companies with significant material weaknesses identified in the Section 404 disclosures potentially have ineffective internal financial reporting controls, which may lead to inaccurate financial statements, hampering shareholders' ability to make informed investment decisions, and may lead to the destruction in public confidence and shareholder value."

3. Executives at some companies have informed the author that their external auditors told them that if they have more than a specified number of control deficiencies, they may not assess their controls as effective. Others have been told that specific deficiencies (e.g., failing to monitor the activities of the database administrator, or failing to have a comprehensive fraud assessment program) are always at least significant and probably material deficiencies. These specific cases are not consistent with the language—and I believe the intent— of AS 5 or the guidance from the SEC. While some may disagree, AS 5 is fundamentally a principles-based standard that emphasizes the use of judgment by both management and the external auditor.

4. In the Introduction to AS 5, the PCAOB states:

> "...the Board has been mindful of the inherent differences in the roles of management and the auditor. Management's daily involvement with its internal control system provides it with knowledge and information that may influence its judgments about how best to evaluate internal control and the sufficiency of the evidence it needs for its annual assessment. Management also should be able to rely on self-assessment and, more generally, the monitoring component of internal control, provided the monitoring component is properly designed and operates effectively.

"The auditor is required to provide an independent opinion on the effectiveness of the company's internal control over financial reporting. The auditor does not have the familiarity with the company's controls that management has and does not interact with or observe these controls with the same frequency as management. Therefore, the auditor cannot obtain sufficient evidence to support an opinion on the effectiveness of internal control based solely on observation of or interaction with the company's controls. Rather, the auditor needs to perform procedures such as inquiry, observation, and inspection of documents, or walkthroughs, which consist of a combination of those procedures, in order to fully understand and identify the likely sources of potential misstatements, while management might be aware of those risk areas on an ongoing basis."

5. In this guide, the terms *material error* and *material misstatement* have been used interchangeably to represent the risk of a material error in the financial statements filed with the SEC, regardless of whether the error is the result of fraud or an inadvertent control failure.

6. In AS 5, the PCAOB used the term *reasonably possible*. In developing the rules for the Section 404 report, the SEC used the term *reasonably likely*, which is also used in the Section 302 certification. In this guide, I use the terms synonymously to mean more than remote but less than probable.

7. The SEC's final rule, *Management's Report on Internal Control Over Financial Reporting and Certification of Disclosure in Exchange Act Reports*, effective August 2003, says:

"...we have modified the final requirements to specify that management must base its evaluation of the effectiveness of the company's internal control over financial reporting on a suitable, recognized control framework that is established by a body or group that has followed due-process procedures, including the broad distribution of the framework for public comment.

"The COSO Framework satisfies our criteria and may be used as an evaluation framework for purposes of management's annual internal control evaluation and disclosure requirements. However, the final rules do not mandate use of a particular framework, such as the COSO Framework, in recognition of the fact that other evaluation standards exist outside of the United States, and that frameworks other than COSO may be developed within the United States in the future, that satisfy the intent of the statute without diminishing the benefits to investors."

8.   In the Introduction to the Standard, paragraph 3.

9.   *Report On The Second-Year Implementation Of Auditing Standard No. 2, An Audit Of Internal Control Over Financial Reporting Performed In Conjunction With An Audit Of Financial Statements*, PCAOB Release No. 2007–004, April 18, 2007.

10. The user of the Sarbanes-Oxley assessment should understand that the quality of the system of internal control as of the reporting date is only an *indication* of future results and depends, among other matters, on there being no significant change to the ICFR. It should be noted that the PCAOB requires (in AS 5) that the report of the external auditors include the following statement: "Projections of any evaluation of effectiveness to future periods are subject to the risk that controls may become inadequate because of changes in conditions, or that the degree of compliance with the policies or procedures may deteriorate."

11. In their *2011 Sarbanes-Oxley Compliance Survey*, available at http://www.protiviti.com/soxsurvey.

12. See the earlier footnote. My recommendation is to use a period of 12 months. However, the SEC and PCAOB have not publicly commented on whether this is the appropriate period.

13. In 2009, a study published in the *CPA Journal* found that the PCAOB had anticipated Sarbanes-Oxley-related audit fees dropping by as much as 10 percent. The authors of the study examined actual audit fee data and found, on average, total audit-related fees dropped by a smaller percentage, estimated at 5 percent (which was offset by increases in hourly rates). However, this includes companies with material weaknesses that were not able to obtain much advantage from the new auditing standard. http://www.allbusiness.com/legal/administrative-law-regulatory-compliance/12285911-1.html.

14. The SEC provided guidance in its January 2002 FAQ number 22 that a formal evaluation of internal controls (similar to that required for Section 404) is not required by current regulations to complete the section 302 certification.

CHAPTER 1 SECTION 404: RULES OR PRINCIPLES

1.   Small businesses and foreign filers will use the equivalent forms 10KSB and 20-F.

2. It is notable that the U.S. Foreign Corrupt Practices Act of 1977 directed that internal controls are the responsibility of management.

3. Initially published in 1992 and an addendum added in 1994, the COSO Internal Control Framework was updated in 2013. The major change was the addition of 17 principles together with guidance in the form of "points of focus." COSO also published *Internal Control over Financial Reporting: Guidance for Smaller Public Companies* in 2006, and in 2004 published *Enterprise Risk Management – Integrated Framework*. The ERM framework did not replace but incorporated the internal control framework. While COSO has indicated that the ERM framework can be used to "satisfy their internal control needs," and even though some companies have selected COSO ERM as the framework to use for Sarbanes-Oxley, it has not been recognized by the SEC as an internal control framework that meets the requirements for Sarbanes-Oxley.

CHAPTER 2 INTERNATIONAL VERSIONS OF SARBANES-OXLEY

1. The reference framework was published in 2010 and is available at http://www.amf-france.org/documents/general/9628_1.pdf.

CHAPTER 3 REVISITING THE PRINCIPLES OF INTERNAL CONTROL

1. AS 5's definition is based on that in COSO 1992, as is that in Codification of Statements on Auditing Standards §319 ('Auditing Standards §319').

2. Securities Exchange Act Rules 13a-15(f) and 15d-15(f).

3. The 5 percent reference is based on the external auditors' general use of a range of 5 percent to 10 percent when determining whether the likelihood of a material error is "more than remote." While it is not generally possible to calculate the probability of an error with any degree of precision, and there is no authoritative guidance in this area, this range is helpful in providing management with a feel for the level of probability being discussed.

4. COBIT 5 is available at www.isaca.org/cobit.

5. The three volumes are an Executive Summary, Framework, and Illustrative Tools. The Executive Summary can be downloaded at no charge from www.coso.org.

CHAPTER 5 WHO IS RESPONSIBLE FOR INTERNAL CONTROLS?

1. This is described further in *A Framework for Internal Auditing's Entitywide Opinion on Internal Control* (The IIA Research Foundation, 2004) and *Internal Audit Reporting Relationships: Serving Two Masters* (The IIA Research Foundation, 2003).

CHAPTER 6 WHAT IS THE SCOPE OF MANAGEMENT'S ASSESSMENT OF THE SYSTEM OF INTERNAL CONTROL OVER FINANCIAL REPORTING?

1. First mentioned in an SEC release in August 2002 and incorporated into the U.S. Securities Exchange Act of 1934 (as amended) Rules 13a-15(e) and 15d-15(e).

2. In its October 2004 *Frequently Asked Questions* report, the SEC addressed in question 23 whether the assessment of ICFR included required supplementary schedules. As indicated below, its conclusion was that the assessment does not currently need to be included within the scope of that assessment.

   "Q: The Commission's rules implementing Section 404, announced in Release No. 34-47986, require management to perform an assessment of internal control over financial reporting which includes the 'preparation of financial statements for external purposes in accordance with generally accepted accounting principles.' Does management's assessment under the Commission's rule specifically require management to assess internal control over financial reporting of required supplementary information? Supplementary information includes the financial statement schedules required by Regulation S-X and any supplementary disclosures required by the FASB. One of the most common examples of such supplementary information is certain disclosures required by the FASB Standard No. 69, Disclosures about Oil and Gas Producing Activities.

   "A: Adequate internal controls over the preparation of supplementary information are required and therefore should be in place and assessed regularly by management. The Commission's rules in Release No. 34-47986 did not specifically address whether the supplementary information should be included in management's assessment of internal control over financial reporting under Section 404. A question has been raised as to whether the supplementary information included in the financial statements should be encompassed in the scope of management's report on their assessment of internal control over financial reporting.

"The Commission staff is considering this question for possible rule making. Additionally, the Commission staff is evaluating broader issues relating to oil and gas disclosures and will include in its evaluation whether rulemaking in this area may be appropriate. Should there be any proposed changes to the current requirements in this area, they will be subject to the Commission's standard rule-making procedures, including a public notice and comment period in advance of rule making. As a result, internal control over the preparation of this supplementary information need not be encompassed in management's assessment of internal control over financial reporting until such time that the Commission has completed its evaluation of this area and issues new rules addressing such requirements."

3. Current reports include Form 6-K, definitive proxy materials, and definitive information statements.

4. In its final rules implementing Section 404, the SEC made the following comments related to the difference between internal controls over financial reporting and disclosure controls. Please note the highlighted section:

"We agree that some components of internal control over financial reporting will be included in disclosure controls and procedures for all companies. *In particular, disclosure controls and procedures will include those components of internal control over financial reporting that provide reasonable assurances that transactions are recorded as necessary to permit preparation of financial statements in accordance with generally accepted accounting principles.* However, in designing their disclosure controls and procedures, companies can be expected to make judgments regarding the processes on which they will rely to meet applicable requirements. In doing so, *some companies might design their disclosure controls and procedures so that certain components of internal control over financial reporting pertaining to the accurate recording of transactions and disposition of assets or to the safeguarding of assets are not included.* For example, a company might have developed internal control over financial reporting that includes as a component of safeguarding of assets dual signature requirements or limitations on signature authority on checks. That company could nonetheless determine that this component is not part of disclosure controls and procedures. *We therefore believe that while there is substantial overlap between internal control over financial reporting and disclosure controls and procedures, many companies will design their disclosure controls and procedures so that they do not include all components of internal control over financial reporting.*"

I concur with the SEC's observation that the referenced controls could be part of a company's system of internal control and yet not be included in disclosure controls. However:

- As noted by the SEC, disclosure controls will include all the components of internal control over financial reporting required to provide reasonable assurance over the reliability of the financial statements. By definition, those are key controls.

- The controls that the SEC has referenced as examples of controls that are included in ICFR, but excluded from disclosure controls, would *not* be considered key controls for Section 404 purposes.

Therefore, while the SEC's position is that there is only "substantial overlap" between ICFR and disclosure controls, in practice, I believe there will be few situations where key controls for Section 404 are not included in disclosure controls.

Some experts, including certain specialized attorneys, have taken a different approach. Arguments include:

- Disclosure controls only relate to the design of controls and not to their operation. If a material weakness relates only to the operation of a control (i.e., it is adequately designed, but not consistently followed), these experts believe management can report an ineffective system of internal control for Section 404, but an effective system of disclosure controls for Section 302. However, we believe such a determination is likely to confuse rather than inform investors.

- Safeguarding of assets is included in the scope of internal controls for Section 404 but not in disclosure controls for Section 302. However, ICFR for Section 404 relates to controls that prevent or detect a misstatement of the financials. A misstatement of the financials filed with the SEC is, by definition, within the scope of disclosure controls.

5. Management may want to consult with SEC counsel on this matter. As discussed in note 13[i], the SEC and certain SEC counsel believe (and I concur) there are aspects of ICFR that are not included in disclosure controls. However, I believe all key controls for Sarbanes-Oxley will be included. An analysis of filings with the SEC in year one of Section 404 identified that 94 percent of the companies that assessed their ICFR as ineffective also assessed their disclosure controls as ineffective.

6. In this guide, the term *interim assessment* of internal controls or disclosure controls is used to refer to what the SEC describes as the *periodic evaluation* of those controls.

CHAPTER 7 DEFINING THE DETAILED SCOPE FOR SARBANES-OXLEY

1. See chapter 7 for a discussion of financial assertions.

2. Paragraph C5 on page A-135 of the standard.

3. Some companies and external auditors have considered materiality relative to interim financial statements when defining significant accounts. In its May 2005 Staff Report, the SEC made it clear that:

    "Companies generally should determine the accounts included within their Section 404 assessment by focusing on annual and company measures rather than interim or segment measures. If management identifies a deficiency when it tests a control, however, at that point it must measure the significance of the deficiency by using both quarterly and annual measures, also considering segment measures where applicable."

4. AS 5 describes significant accounts and disclosures as having "a reasonable possibility of containing misstatements that would cause the financial statements to be materially misstated."

5. In the first few years of Sarbanes-Oxley assessments, on the advice of the external auditor, many companies adopted a lower measure called *planning materiality*. They would establish materiality at 5 percent of pre-tax income and then a lower level—perhaps half that number—as planning materiality. In some cases, they took a further "haircut" based on perceived risk levels—perhaps another 10 percent—to establish planning materiality. All accounts above planning materiality would then be determined to be significant accounts.

This is no longer seen as appropriate, as it brings into scope accounts where there is less than a reasonable possibility of a material error.

Other companies have decided that using a reduced materiality level, similar to planning materiality, is advisable because it is prudent. While ensuring that there are adequate controls to prevent or detect errors that are less than material is a sound objective, there is no need to include these accounts in scope and subject to external auditor testing. My advice is to include in scope only significant accounts as described in this guide. Key controls over the smaller accounts may be described as *key business controls*, subject to periodic testing by management or the internal auditor.

6.   Appendix B, under Multiple Locations Scoping Decisions.

7.   Available at http://www.sec.gov/info/accountants/controlfaq.htm.

8.   The PCAOB has removed the requirement from AS 5, previously in AS 2, to understand key business processes and transactions. This is to allow flexibility in approach by the external auditor. I include it in the guide because I have found this approach valuable in practice.

9.   *Report On The Initial Implementation Of Auditing Standard No. 2, An Audit Of Internal Control Over Financial Reporting Performed In Conjunction With An Audit Of Financial Statements.*

10.   *Thinking outside the SOX box: transforming your compliance function for competitive advantage.* http://www.ey.com/Publication/vwLUAssets/ Think_outside_the_SOX_box:_Transform_your_compliance_function_for_ competitive_advantage/$FILE/Thinking%20outside%20the%20box.pdf.

11.   Note: Some of the external audit firms emphasize a concept called *key reports*, which are commonly described as reports used in key controls. However, I believe the only key reports that need to be examined, as automated controls, are those where an error would not be detected in the normal course of the manual part of the control.

12.   The IIA's *Guide to the Assessment of IT General Controls Scope Based on Risk* was first published in January 2007. In its first six months, GAIT was downloaded nearly 10,000 times and its use is becoming widespread, not only within the United States, but also in Europe and Asia. Through the end of 2010, the methodology has been downloaded 36,000 times. GAIT was updated to reflect changes in PCAOB and SEC guidance in August 2007 and can be found on The IIA's website at http://www.theiia.org/guidance/technology/gait/gait-m/.

13. According to an EY study, 51 percent of companies have more issues (control failures) with IT general controls than any other area.

14. In its guidance for management, the SEC uses the term *critical functionality* to refer to all functionality relied upon that is not an automated control (text in footnotes in the SEC document have been replaced by text in parentheses):

"Controls that management identifies as addressing financial reporting risks may be automated (for example, application controls that perform automated matching, error checking, or edit checking functions), dependent upon IT functionality (for example, consistent application of a formula or performance of a calculation and posting correct balances to appropriate accounts or ledgers), or a combination of both manual and automated procedures (for example, a control that manually investigates items contained in a computer generated exception report). In these situations, management's evaluation process generally considers the design and operation of the automated or IT-dependent application controls and the relevant IT general controls over the applications providing the IT functionality. While IT general controls alone ordinarily do not adequately address financial reporting risks, the proper and consistent operation of automated controls or IT functionality often depends upon effective IT general controls. The identification of risks and controls within IT should not be a separate evaluation. Instead, it should be an integral part of management's top-down, risk-based approach to identifying risks and controls and in determining evidential matter necessary to support the assessment.

"Aspects of IT general controls that may be relevant to the evaluation of ICFR will vary depending upon a company's facts and circumstances. For purposes of the evaluation of ICFR, management only needs to evaluate those IT general controls that are necessary for the proper and consistent operation of other controls designed to adequately address financial reporting risks. For example, management might consider whether certain aspects of IT general control areas, such as program development, program changes, computer operations, and access to programs and data, apply to its facts and circumstances. Specifically, it is unnecessary to evaluate IT general controls that primarily pertain to efficiency or effectiveness of a company's operations, but which are not relevant to addressing financial reporting risks."

15. One example of specialized software for models is SAS.

16. Management can reference the PCAOB's answer to question 24 on service organizations in its *Staff Questions and Answers,* issued on June 23, 2004.

17. Paragraph 24 of Auditing Standard No. 2.

18. SAS 99 makes a similar statement: "For purposes of the Statement, fraud is an intentional act that results in a material misstatement in financial statements that are the subject of an audit."

19. Fraud is assumed in this discussion to include the misappropriation of assets.

20. The IIA, AICPA, and the Association of Certified Fraud Examiners (ACFE) collaborated on *Managing the Business Risk of Fraud: A Practical Guide* in 2008.

CHAPTER 8 TESTING KEY CONTROLS

1. Some companies have gained efficiencies by conducting joint walkthroughs with the external auditors; this is more likely when the management testing is performed by the internal audit function.

CHAPTER 9 ASSESSING THE ADEQUACY OF CONTROLS, INCLUDING ASSESSING DEFICIENCIES

1. As noted earlier, the key to an aggregated risk is that the controls are likely to fail at the same time because, for instance, they are performed at the same time by the same people, or using the same computer system.

2. The framework was developed by nine CPA firms (BDO Seidman LLP, Crowe Chizek and Company LLC, Deloitte & Touche LLP, Ernst & Young LLP, Grant Thornton LLP, Harbinger PLC, KPMG LLP, McGladrey & Pullen LLP, and PricewaterhouseCoopers LLP) in association with a respected academic. It can be found at http://www.gellerco.com/docs/SO_Framework_V3.pdf.

3. Detailed guidance in the assessment of ITGC deficiencies can be found in *GAIT for IT General Control Deficiency Assessment* at www.theiia.org/guidance/technology.

4. I recommend consulting with SEC counsel, although it appears reasonable to assume that if a material weakness is material to the investor, then its resolution is highly likely to be a material change in the system of internal controls—and

similarly likely to be material to the investor. In January 2002, SEC staff issued answers to a number of Frequently Asked Questions. The answer to question 22 is relevant, and key portions are highlighted in the extract below:

"Although proposed amendments to Exchange Act Rules 13a-15 and 15d-15 would impose a requirement on an issuer's management to conduct an evaluation, with the participation of the issuer's CEO and CFO, of the effectiveness of the issuer's internal controls and procedures for financial reporting…, the Commission's rules currently do not specifically require an issuer's CEO or CFO, or the issuer itself, to conduct periodic evaluations of the issuer's internal controls or the issuer's internal controls and procedures for financial reporting. Some elements of internal controls are included in the definition of disclosure controls and procedures. There is a current evaluation requirement involving the CEO and the CFO of that portion of internal controls that is included within disclosure controls and procedures as part of the required evaluation of disclosure controls and procedures. We expect that issuers generally also would engage in an evaluation of internal controls. We believe that issuers generally currently evaluate internal controls, for example, in connection with reviewing compliance with Section 13(b) of the Exchange Act or in connection with the preparation or audit of financial statements.

"…to the extent that an issuer has conducted an evaluation of its internal controls as of the end of the period covered by the report, including under the circumstances described in the preceding paragraph, *the issuer should disclose any significant changes to the internal controls* or in other factors that could significantly affect these controls subsequent to the date of their evaluation, *including any corrective actions with regard to significant deficiencies and material weaknesses*. If the issuer has made any significant changes to internal controls or in other factors that could significantly affect these controls, such changes would presumably follow some evaluation, in which case the required disclosure must be made."

CHAPTER 11 USING TECHNOLOGY IN THE SARBANES-OXLEY PROGRAM

1. There are a great many vendors with a variety of functionality offered in their solutions. The vendors range from the large, enterprise application software vendors like SAP and Oracle to smaller vendors like Approva, BWise, and others.

CHAPTER 13 AN EFFICIENT SYSTEM OF INTERNAL CONTROL OVER FINANCIAL REPORTING

1. One often-used source of process metrics is the Hackett Group (http://www.thehackettgroup.com/process-metrics/).

CHAPTER 15 THE ROLE OF INTERNAL AUDIT

1. *State of the internal audit profession study: internal audit post Sarbanes-Oxley.*

2. *Optimizing the Role of Internal Audit in the Sarbanes-Oxley Era Second Edition* (2006).

3. *How to rebalance internal audit priorities in the Sarbanes-Oxley era* (2005).

CHAPTER 16 THE RELATIONSHIP BETWEEN GOVERNANCE, RISK MANAGEMENT, AND COMPLIANCE: ERM; AND SARBANES-OXLEY

1. The OCEG *Red Book* is available for download at http://www.oceg.org/view/RB2Project.

2. OCEG defines *Principled Performance* (a registered trademark of OCEG) as "the outcome of clearly articulating an enterprise's objectives, both financial and nonfinancial, and defining the methods by which it establishes and stays within the boundaries it will observe while staying driving towards those objectives. Principled Performance is achieved by defining 'right' for your company, then doing the 'right' things the 'right' way—not only to create value in the traditional view, but to protect value, address uncertainty and help the organization stay within its customized boundaries of conduct."